Marcus Aurelius

LOWER
GERMANIA   *CHATTI*

BELGICA

UPPER
GERMANIA   MARCOMANNI

GALLIA   CARPATHIAN MOUNTAINS

          RAETIA   QUADI
THE ALPS   Vindobona •Carnuntum
          NORICUM   •Aquincum
ALPES   Aquileia UPPER LOWER   *IAZYGES*
          Altinum•   PANNONIA PANNONIA
          Po   DACIA
          Ravenna•   Sirmium• Danube

          ITALY   Adriatic Sea DALMATIA   MOESIA

          •Rome   THRACE
          Capua•   •Canusium   MACEDONIA   Cyzicus•
    Sardinia   Brundisium•   Aegean Pergamum
                                        Sea   •ASIA
                              EPIRUS   Smyr•
    Carthage•   *Sicily*   Eleusis• Ephesus•
                              ACHAEA Athens
    AFRICA

                Crete

          Mediterranean Sea

                    •Cyrene
              CYRENE

          ▨ Roman Empire

The map excludes the western edge of the empire,
which Marcus Aurelius never visited and which
is seldom mentioned in this biography.

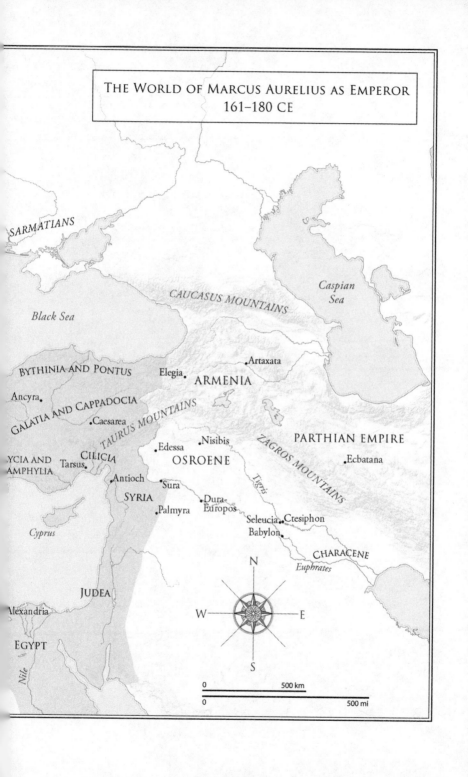

THE WORLD OF MARCUS AURELIUS AS EMPEROR
161–180 CE

SARMATIANS

Black Sea

CAUCASUS MOUNTAINS

Caspian Sea

BYTHINIA AND PONTUS

Elegia

ARMENIA

Artaxata

Ancyra

GALATIA AND CAPPADOCIA

Caesarea

TAURUS MOUNTAINS

PARTHIAN EMPIRE

Nisibis

ZAGROS MOUNTAINS

Ecbatana

YCIA AND AMPHYLIA

Tarsus

CILICIA

Edessa

OSROENE

Antioch

Sura

SYRIA

Palmyra

Dura-Europos

Tigris

Seleucia

Ctesiphon

Babylon

Cyprus

CHARACENE

Euphrates

JUDEA

Alexandria

EGYPT

Nile

N

W   E

S

0   500 km
0   500 mi

Marcus Aurelius

The Stoic Emperor

Donald J. Robertson

· ANCIENT LIVES ·

Yale

UNIVERSITY PRESS

NEW HAVEN & LONDON

Published with assistance from the foundation established in memory of
Amasa Stone Mather of the Class of 1907, Yale College.

Yale University Press books may be purchased in quantity for
educational, business, or promotional use. For information, please e-mail
sales.press@yale.edu (U.S. office) or sales@yaleup.co.uk (U.K. office).

Frontispiece: Beehive Mapping.

Set in the Yale typeface designed by Matthew Carter, and Louize,
designed by Matthieu Cortat, by Integrated Publishing Solutions.
Printed in the United States of America.

Library of Congress Control Number: 2023939888
ISBN 978-0-300-25666-6 (hardcover : alk. paper)
ISBN 978-0-300-28014-2 (paperback)

A catalogue record for this book is available from the British Library.

10 9 8 7 6 5 4 3 2 1

· ANCIENT LIVES ·

Ancient Lives unfolds the stories of thinkers, writers, kings, queens, conquerors, and politicians from all parts of the ancient world. Readers will come to know these figures in fully human dimensions, complete with foibles and flaws, and will see that the issues they faced — political conflicts, constraints based in gender or race, tensions between the private and public self — have changed very little over the course of millennia.

James Romm
Series Editor

For Poppy, for history and philosophy combined

Contents

Contents

Marcus Aurelius

Prologue

TRUTH IN THE *MEDITATIONS*

M arcus Aurelius did not have a heart of stone. When the news was brought to him that one of his most beloved tutors had died, the young Caesar was distraught, and tears poured down his cheeks — he may perhaps have started to beat his chest and tear his clothes in grief. Palace servants, afraid his reputation would be harmed by such a public display of raw emotion, rushed to his side, trying to restrain him. His adoptive father, the emperor Antoninus Pius, a thoughtful and gentle man, gestured for them to step aside. He whispered, "Let him be only a man for once; for neither philosophy nor empire takes away natural feeling."[1]

Such displays of emotion were not out of character for Marcus. We hear of him in his fifties, as emperor, being moved to tears when an advocate giving a speech uttered the words, "Blessed are those who died in the plague!"[2] Toward the end of his life, the emperor likewise found himself weeping over a letter informing him that a catastrophic earthquake had leveled the city of Smyrna (modern-day Izmir, Turkey). His tears soaked the parchment as he read, "She is a desert through which the west winds blow."[3] He was a man capable of knowing intense grief. Perhaps especially for that reason, he committed himself to a lifelong training in philosophy: Marcus came to realize that although a great leader may experience sorrow or anger, he cannot allow intense emotion to cloud his judgment.

Throughout his personal notebooks, known today as the *Meditations*, Marcus returns many times to one central question: How can we prevent reason from being usurped by the passions? If we focus on what is before us, he concluded, following reason from moment to moment "with heroic truth in every word," we will be achieving the goal of life.[4] The pages of the *Meditations* show its writer again and again striving to maintain a rational and brutally honest attitude toward life's most troubling events, from personal tragedies, such as the loss of his beloved tutor, to international catastrophes, such as the great wars that Rome faced during his time as emperor.

This was no bookish or academic philosophy but rather a way of life. The love of truth was almost a religion to Marcus. The divine Nature of the universe and all that exists, he believed to be synonymous with a primordial goddess named Truth, or Aletheia.[5] Liars and the self-deceived are guilty of *impiety* because they place themselves at odds with divine Nature. The philosopher who lives in accord with truth, by contrast, is "like a priest and minister of the gods."[6] Indeed, Rome's emperor held the office of pontifex maximus, supreme priest. Marcus doubtless saw his commitment to philosophical truth as an integral part of fulfilling his religious obligations, both as an individual and as the head of state.

He was, moreover, a student of *human* nature whose search for truth extended to the lives of others, even leading him to experiment with writing biographies. As a young man, he sought the guidance of his rhetoric master on the methods to employ in composing a history.[7] In addition to his own memoirs he began work on his *Acts of Ancient Greeks and Romans*, though he eventually scrapped both projects.[8] Studying the character of others became a contemplative exercise for him; as he writes in the *Meditations*, "Accustom yourself to attend carefully to what is said by another, and as much as it is possible, be in the speaker's mind."[9]

We can perhaps see evidence of Marcus's own character evolving in his writings. The lively and good-humored letters of his youth focus on his studies in rhetoric and the trivia of daily life – aches and pains, family vacations, squabbles among his friends. It is hard to reconcile them with the author, decades later, of the *Meditations*, which strikes a more solemn and reflective note. (Although, to some extent this is to be expected as the *Meditations* is a different type of writing.) Perhaps we can detect a similar transformation in various sculptures made of him during his lifetime. In his prime, some show him arching his eyebrows, as if considering a problem with studied logic. In others, his eyes are turned dreamily upward, as though contemplating the heavens.[10] Statues portraying the emperor toward the end of his life present him gazing dead ahead, his features fallen into a look of solemn resignation. The former befit an aspiring philosopher, the latter a seasoned military commander who has lived through war after war and witnessed a horrific plague.

If we are going to enter the mind of the Stoic emperor, however, we need to consider the evidence of his thoughts and actions carefully. Marcus had a philosophy of life which differs significantly from the prevailing values of any modern society. Some of his recent biographers have dealt rather dismissively with the Stoic philosophy that played such an important role in his life: "A more priggish, inhuman, killjoy and generally repulsive doctrine [than Stoicism] would be hard to imagine," sneers one, "but it will be abundantly clear why the programme appealed to Marcus Aurelius."[11] Such a view of Stoicism is a caricature based on popular misconceptions, and it does the philosophy no justice. Stoicism flourished for five centuries in the ancient world, and numerous proponents spoke to its benefits and appeal. Today thousands of psychological research studies provide scientific evidence for the effectiveness of modern cognitive psychotherapy, which was originally inspired by the Stoics.[12] Many modern readers likewise find in Stoicism a profoundly life-changing philosophy — one which heals certain emotions rather than merely eliminating all of them.

Trying to write a biography of Marcus Aurelius without due attention to the influence of Stoicism would, indeed, be as absurd as trying to write about Saint Augustine while ignoring his Christian faith. Marcus was engaged in a process of both moral and therapeutic self-improvement. We cannot understand his character without understanding why Stoicism became so important to him and how it shaped his actions. In this book I aim, therefore, to weave together evidence of his inner thoughts and values, found in his private notes and letters, with evidence of his outward actions, taken from Roman historians and other ancient sources.

Most readers are interested in Marcus because of the famous book attributed to him. The *Meditations* has become one of the most cherished self-improvement classics of all time. It has had a profound influence on countless individuals throughout history, from all walks of life. Modern appreciation of the *Meditations* began when the first printed edition of the Greek manuscript was published in 1558, bearing the title "To himself" (*Ta eis heauton*), along with a Latin translation. In 1634, the first English translation appeared under the title *Marcus Aurelius Antoninus the Roman Emperor, His Meditations Concerning Himself...*[13] The use of this term eventually stuck, and it is now common therefore to title the book simply *Meditations*.

So what are the core teachings "to himself" that Marcus Aurelius set down in the *Meditations*? Most important is "living in agreement with Nature," which the Stoics defined as humanity's supreme goal. Although Marcus uses the word "Stoic" only once, he often cites this central maxim of their philosophy. He gives thanks that his Stoic tutors provided him with frequent examples of what "living in agreement with Nature" meant in practice, in their daily lives. He also tells himself that nothing can prevent him from living in agreement with Nature, just as they did, although he often struggled to do so in practice.[14]

Living "in agreement with Nature," for the Stoics, meant living *rationally*, because they considered reason to be the highest human faculty. If we lived consistently in accord with reason, we would perfect our nature and attain the virtue of wisdom. If we applied such wisdom in our relationships with others, treating them honestly and fairly, we would achieve the *social* virtue of justice. In order to live more fully in accord with wisdom and justice, though, we need to master the fears and desires that threaten to lead us astray. This calls for courage and moderation, giving us the four cardinal virtues of ancient Stoicism: wisdom, justice, fortitude, and temperance. The Stoic goal of life can be understood in this sense as "living in accord with virtue," as long as we bear in mind that the Stoics took all the virtues to be forms of moral wisdom.

Although the wise are not highly perturbed by misfortune, neither are they completely unfeeling. Marcus Aurelius, as we've seen, could be a sensitive man. He gradually trained himself to manage his emotions by examining them rationally rather than merely suppressing them. Stoicism taught him to view external events — events beyond his direct control – as of secondary importance. He learned a kind of psychological therapy, designed to free him from unhealthy passions, a state of mind called *apatheia* by the Stoics. (The word in Stoic philosophy is closer to "freedom from pathological emotions" than what we mean today by "apathy.") Almost everything Marcus says about philosophy can be related back to the basic goal of living in agreement with Nature, free of unhealthy emotions. Throughout this book I have interspersed more than a hundred such citations from the *Meditations* to highlight the connections between its author's Stoic principles and the way he actually conducted himself in life.

Who was Marcus Aurelius the man, though? Many today came to know him through his portrayal by Richard Harris in the movie *Gladiator* (2000), and a few may recall Alec Guinness in *The Fall of the Roman Empire* (1964) – but these films are only loosely based on history. As it happens, we know more about Marcus Aurelius's biography than that of any other Stoic or of almost any other ancient philosopher. Three main Roman histories survive that describe his life and character: the *Roman History* of Cassius Dio, the *History of the Empire from the Death of Marcus* by Herodian, and the multi-author *Augustan History*.[15] We also possess a cache of private letters between Marcus and his rhetoric tutor Marcus Cornelius Fronto that give us exceptional insight into his private life as Caesar (designated heir of the emperor) and later as emperor himself. (These and other sources are described in more detail in the Source Notes.)

In these sources, we encounter colorful characters with whose lives Marcus Aurelius's story was intertwined. The emperor Hadrian, for instance, features prominently in this book because he had a profound influence on the boy's upbringing. Marcus Aurelius was born under Hadrian's rule, later adopted as his grandson, and even brought to live in his villa during the final months of Hadrian's life. Hadrian has a reputation today as one of the better emperors, which he owes in part to Marguerite Yourcenar's celebrated novel *Memoirs of Hadrian:* as one of his other biographers notes, "It is no exaggeration to say that for a while Mme. Yourcenar supplanted the academics. Her Hadrian was received as a true image of the real thing."[16] Yourcenar's book, considered by many to be a literary masterpiece, draws on careful research. It was, however, intended as a work of historical fiction, and it portrays Hadrian far more sympathetically than is justified by the historical evidence. It is written from Hadrian's perspective in the form of letters from him to the young Marcus Aurelius, whose replies we never see. The book you are currently reading is more concerned with that boy's story – and Marcus Aurelius had nothing positive to say about Hadrian.

Hadrian's name is conspicuously absent from book 1 of the *Meditations,* which lists the sixteen family members and tutors whose qualities Marcus most admires. That book is, in a sense, his *autobiography,* though perhaps it would be better to call it a fragment of an autobiography, as the author tells us only how specific individuals inspired him. He leaves out the others, such as the many critics of his rule who opposed him or came to see him as their enemy. He also omits virtually any reference to the major events of his life. In this modern biography I build on these fragments, and other sources, to show how Marcus took inspiration from his family and his tutors as a young man, and how he proceeded to apply the Stoic philosophy they taught him to the enormous challenges he faced as emperor.

CHAPTER ONE

The Mother of Caesar

"Piety and kindness," writes his frail hand, listing qualities the author learned from his mother, "and abstinence not only from evil deeds, but even from evil thoughts."[1] Marcus Aurelius is in his fifties. It is late at night and the frigid winter air of Aquincum (modern-day Budapest) has brought on his familiar hacking cough. As usual, he has difficulty sleeping. Outside the *praetorium*, his headquarters at the center of the legionary fortress, everything is deceptively silent. The Praetorians, his personal regiment, are camped in nearby barracks. The whole empire has been devastated by a horrific pandemic, which would eventually be named the Antonine Plague, after Marcus Aurelius Antoninus's imperial dynasty. The First Marcomannic War still rages along the Danube frontier. The army is exhausted from fighting one battle after another against the enemy tribes, the Quadi and Iazyges, on the other side of the river. In the midst of all these troubles, the emperor is writing his personal notes on the application of Stoic philosophy. He pauses momentarily to gaze upon a wood-panel portrait of Lucilla, his mother. Slowly turning over the lesson that he learned from her half a century earlier, he must have asked himself, How can a man learn to abstain even from the very *thought* of doing wrong?

Domitia Lucilla, also known as Domitia Calvilla, gave birth to her first child, Marcus Annius Verus—the future Roman emperor Marcus Aurelius—on April 26, 121 CE. His only sibling, a sister named Annia Cornificia Faustina, arrived a year later. The children were born into a wealthy patrician family with close ties to Hadrian, the ruling emperor. Later, Marcus would study under several of Rome's finest rhetoricians and philosophers, but Lucilla, his mother, would have been his first teacher.

They were clearly very close. Long before Marcus began any formal education, his mother had sown within him the seeds of a love for Greek literature and philosophy. She also taught him to pay close attention to his thoughts and look deep within himself, examining his own motives and values. Doing good outwardly is not enough; the real goal of life is to be good in ourselves.

"Look within. Within is the fountain of good, and it will ever bubble up, if you will ever dig."[2]

Lucilla's early concern with moral self-examination bore fruit for her son throughout his life, but most notably decades later, when he began writing the *Meditations*.

"My little mother," Marcus calls her affectionately in his letters, but she must have commanded great respect as one of the wealthiest and most powerful women in Rome. From her parents she had inherited extensive clay fields, and a large brick-and-tile factory on the banks of the Tiber, which had produced the materials used in the construction of the Colosseum, Pantheon, and Market of Trajan. Archaeologists have unearthed many bricks with her name stamped on them; it would appear that Marcus's "little mother" was one of the leading magnates of the Roman construction industry at the start of the second century CE. Marcus admired her exceptional generosity (today we would call her a philanthropist), and he later expressed gratitude that thanks to her he had the resources to help those who were short of money or needed other forms of assistance.[3]

Marcus grew up around his mother's circle of friends, who included some of the leading intellectuals in the empire. Lucilla was a natural Hellenophile. Indeed, her side of the family claimed descent from a legendary king, Malemnius, who founded a prominent city on Italy's Salentine peninsula, Lupiae, where Greek colonists had settled in the distant past. (The surrounding region to this day retains strong cultural ties to Greece.) Roman Hellenism ran in her veins, and she was known for her exceptional grasp of the Greek language. Fluency in Greek had been fashionable since the latter part of Nero's reign, half a century earlier, when Rome experienced the renaissance in the appreciation of Greek culture known as the Second Sophistic. The Sophists were Greek orators who discussed literature with their students but also claimed to impart moral lessons about virtue. Hence, the word *sophistication,* the quality that the parents of young Roman nobles hoped their sons might acquire from foreign intellectuals. Although most wealthy Romans at this time were bilingual in the two languages, Lucilla's exceptional mastery of Greek is evident. Marcus Cornelius Fronto, the preeminent Latin rhetorician of his day, wrote letters in Greek addressed "To the Mother of Caesar" and somewhat pathetically begged Marcus to proofread one: "I have written your mother a letter, such is my assurance, in Greek, and enclose it in my letter to you. Please read it first, and if you detect any barbarism in it, for you are fresher from your Greek than I am, correct it and so hand it over to your mother. I should not like her to look down on me as a goth."[4]

Marcus had close ties with the Second Sophistic through Lucilla's side of the family. Her maternal (adoptive) grandfather, Lucius Catilius Severus, a military veteran and senior Roman statesman favored by the emperor, was a major patron of the Sophists. Catilius also took special interest in the education of his family. Owing to his generosity, Marcus received instruction at home from the finest private tutors, rather than depending on public lectures.[5] Foremost among their circle was the celebrated Greek orator Herodes Atticus, who was raised in the household of Marcus's great-grandfather. Lucilla grew up alongside the leading figure of the Second Sophistic, of whom another orator once exclaimed, "O Herodes, we Sophists are all of us merely small slices of yourself!"[6] Marcus had a lifelong respect for the verbal prowess of Herodes and other Greek rhetoricians. As a budding orator, he was bound to compare himself to them. Nevertheless, he would later say that he was grateful that he avoided falling under their spell.

Lucilla was also good friends with Fronto, Herodes' Latin counterpart. Fronto's correspondence mentions Lucilla as a close friend of his young wife, Gratia, whom she evidently took under her wing. They probably read Greek literature together. It is a striking testimony to Marcus's mother that Fronto, one of the empire's most acclaimed teachers, regarded her as a mentor to his own wife. Lucilla simultaneously fostered an intellectual atmosphere in her own household, encouraging her son, and perhaps also her daughter, to associate with artists and thinkers who would shape their character for the rest of their lives.

Although it goes unmentioned in Marcus's brief character sketch of his mother, Lucilla exhibited another notable virtue: *natural affection*. Marcus came to agree with Fronto that generally speaking, "those among us who are called Patricians are rather deficient" in precisely this quality.[7] Wealthy Roman slaveowners and the baying audiences at gladiatorial contests may appear to have been numb to human suffering. However, individuals can always be found who stand apart from their contemporaries. The Greek word Marcus and Fronto used of such people, *philostorgia*, which normally refers to the love of close family members for one another, is central to Stoic ethics. *Philostorgia* is sometimes translated as "natural affection," "parental love," or "familial love," although we might best describe it as resembling the Christian concept of *brotherly* love. Paul equates the two terms in the New Testament: "Be kindly affectionate [*philostorgoi*] to one another with brotherly love [*philadelphia*]."[8]

The Stoics believed that such "natural affection" should extend to everyone, as all rational beings are viewed by the wise as their brothers and sisters. In his letters, Fronto more than once makes the striking claim that the Latin language has no equivalent word for *philostorgia*, as in his description of a friend: "His characteristics, simplicity, continence, truthfulness, and honour plainly Roman, a warmth of affection, however, possibly not Roman, for there is nothing of which my whole life through I have seen less at Rome than a man unfeignedly φιλόστοργος [*philostorgos*]. The reason why there is not even a word for this virtue in our language must, I imagine, be, that in reality no one at Rome has any warm affection."[9] It is clear from Fronto's correspondence that he viewed Marcus and Lucilla as exceptions, among the few patricians in Rome who were capable of exhibiting the natural affection held in such regard by philosophers. Indeed, Marcus's warmth and affection toward his friends is displayed throughout the correspondence with his Latin master. He even praises Fronto, on one occasion, by comparing his eloquence to Lucilla's.[10] She could almost be considered a Sophist herself, were it not that women rarely engaged in public speaking at this time, and her manner appears more plainspoken and less affected than that of the typical Greek rhetorician.

If we can see beyond Fronto's rather shameless toadying, his letters provide us with additional insights into Lucilla's character and her influence upon her son. Fronto celebrates the virtues for which Marcus's mother was known in a letter he sent her on her birthday in which he compares her to Athena, the Greek goddess of wisdom.[11] He portrays Lucilla as a woman known for having had great love, or natural affection, toward her husband, and for loving her children. The letter suggests that she is seen as virtuous yet modest, good-natured, approachable, and kind. She is also portrayed as a straightforward, honest woman. Fronto concludes by saying that he would bar from Lucilla's birthday celebrations any persons who made "a pretense of good-will" and were "insincere," those for whom everything from laughter to tears was make-believe, and who, as Homer's Achilles put it, hid "one thing in their hearts while their lips speak another."[12] He apparently did not see himself in this description, but it surely conjured to mind other rhetoricians of his and Marcus's acquaintance. Fronto would certainly have insisted that Marcus read his mother's birthday letter, so it is likely that its portrayal of her met with her son's approval. Lucilla emerges, in Fronto's highly contrived compliment, as a woman known for her familial affection, her honesty, and, ironically, her straight talking.

Marcus recognized that these qualities clashed at times with the culture of the Second Sophistic, which elevated insincerity and sycophancy to an art form, and Fronto was arguably not much better than the Greek Sophists in this regard. His birthday letter could be dismissed as mere flattery, but it echoes what Marcus said about his mother privately in the *Meditations*. Fronto was right: the woman who taught her son not only to avoid doing wrong but to avoid even contemplating a wrong action inwardly would doubtless "hate like the gates of hell" hypocrites of the sort denounced by Achilles in Homer's *Iliad*. It is no surprise that such a woman would rear a son who became famous for his love of truthfulness.

Much less is known about Marcus's father. He was named Marcus Annius Verus, after his own father. Like Lucilla, he was born into a wealthy and influential senatorial family. They hailed from the Roman province of Hispania Baetica (southern Spain), where they had made their fortune from olive oil. Verus's side of the family claimed descent from Numa Pompilius, the second king of Rome. Renowned as a wise and just ruler, Numa was credited with founding the solemn rites of the Roman religion. A popular tradition, whose historical authenticity was scorned even in antiquity, claimed Numa brought to Rome the teachings of the sixth-century BCE philosopher Pythagoras of Samos, whose Greek followers had settled around the southern tip of the Italian peninsula. Although the Annius Verus family's historical connection with Numa and Pythagoreanism is probably a myth, it reveals something of their character and reputation. Marcus Aurelius was the latest in a line of reputedly peaceful and high-minded nobles with links to archaic religion and philosophy.

Marcus's father also had a touch of imperial blood in his veins. He was not only the nephew of Empress Vibia Sabina, wife of Hadrian, but also a distant relative of Emperor Trajan on his mother's side. His sister Faustina (the Elder) was married to a senator who would later become the emperor Antoninus Pius. Marcus's aunt was therefore destined to become an Augusta, or empress. Given his family history and imperial connections, Marcus's father must have been expected to reach the highest civil office, that of consul. Instead, soon after he reached the preceding rank of praetor, his career was unexpectedly cut short. (The best modern analogy I can think of is that of a man who seems destined to become prime minister and reaches the rank of cabinet minister but is denied the opportunity to achieve his full career potential.)

Sometime in the early 120s, when Marcus was around three or four years old, his father died. We have no more details; we know only that just a few years into her marriage, Lucilla was left a widow caring for two small children. One of our sources claims that "at the beginning of his life" Marcus assumed the name of his maternal great-grandfather, Catilius Severus, which might imply that the old man temporarily adopted him after he lost his father.[13] Lucilla was still a teenager or in her early twenties. She never remarried.

This first tragic loss shaped Marcus's character more than the many others he was to experience. We can detect throughout the rest of his life a constant interplay between his natural sensitivity to grief and a studied philosophical attitude toward his own death and that of others. "Lucilla buried Verus," he writes bluntly of this first tragic loss, looking back on these events half a century later.[14] And so it goes on, he muses, ever the same, with one life after another. His father, Marcus Annius Verus, and all the others were merely "creatures of a day," gone before long. Yet he, Marcus Aurelius, still recalled them and shed tears for them.

Marcus barely had a chance to know his father. Nevertheless, for the rest of his life, following custom, he would pray before this man's image in his family shrine (*lararium*), honoring his memory. Marcus was forced to construct a memory of his father from the fragments of his own childhood recollections and the stories he heard about him. Marcus believed, first and foremost, that his father exemplified both manliness and modesty.[15] Later he asserts that the word "manly" (*arrenikos*), correctly defined, means not being tough and aggressive but kind and full of natural affection. Marcus, I think, remembered his father as the embodiment of a gentle and affectionate man, at odds with the vicious cliques of Roman elite society. Turning to one male role model after another, Marcus struggled to live up to his father's example. Like many troubled young men, his own feelings of anger would at times get in his way.

CHAPTER TWO

Verissimus the Philosopher

After the formal nine days of mourning for her husband were over, Marcus's mother sat by her two young children and explained that their toys were to be packed away by the servants. They were leaving their familiar, beloved home on Rome's Caelian Hill to move into the nearby villa of Marcus's paternal grandfather, who also bore the name Marcus Annius Verus. "When his father died," as the *Augustan History* puts it, young Marcus "was adopted and reared by his father's father."[1] At first the young noble felt some anxiety at the prospect of adjusting to a new way of life – he would later compare the transition to a sort of death.[2] He nevertheless grew to think of his grandfather as another good man, much like his father.

It was this venerable statesman's "nobility of character" and "freedom from anger" that made the most lasting impression on his young grandson.[3] An even-tempered gentleness seemed to run in the Annius Verus family. Yet Marcus's time in this household was not entirely untroubled. Marcus's grandfather was close to Hadrian. Indeed, when the emperor took the throne, in 117 CE, Verus was appointed urban prefect, the senior official in charge of the city of Rome, a position he held for about seven years. Since the end of his grandfather's tenure in this position coincided with the time Marcus's father is believed to have died, it is possible that the old statesman had retired from public office in order to help raise his grandson.

The emperor, meanwhile, traveled extensively throughout the provinces and spent much of this time away from Rome. It must have been when Hadrian was in the city, around 125–128, that young Marcus had first caught his attention. The boy was not only part of a wealthy and influential patrician family and the grandson of one of Rome's most senior statesmen, he was also a grandnephew of the emperor's wife. Marcus soon became a favorite at court and we are told he was reared "in Hadrian's lap" (or "bosom," the Latin gremio).[4]

A few years later, the emperor chose to honor Marcus by enrolling him in the equestrian order, making him a Roman knight at the age of six. The equites, from equus, "horse" (their predecessors were cavalrymen), were Rome's second political stratum, below the senatorial class. Marcus was being prepared for a future role in the upper echelons of Roman society. Soon afterward Hadrian left for Athens, but he had already arranged, astutely, for the boy to be enrolled the following year in a religious order known as the College of the Salii.

The arcane chants and rituals of the Salii fascinated young Marcus. His grandfather must have been proud, knowing that the priesthood traced its origins back to King Numa, their family's legendary ancestor. Marcus joined the other boys who were learning to perform elaborate "leaping" war dances. Their ceremonial dress consisted of bronze cuirasses and embroidered tunics, and they bore archaic shields and daggers.[5] Torches blazed, the air thick with incense, as the Salii threw themselves into the air, thumping their shields hypnotically in time to the martial music. In unison with his fellow priests, Marcus chanted the cryptic verses of their ancient hymn, the *Carmen Saliare*, honoring Mars Gravidus, the god of marching into war.[6]

For years Marcus was a devoted member of this religious dance troupe, eventually becoming its leader. Decades later, in the *Meditations*, he seems at times to be drawing on his memories of these days. Some commit themselves so wholeheartedly to dance, he writes, that they exhaust themselves, even going without food and sleep, as they work obsessively to perfect their art.[7] He asks himself why it seems so difficult, then, to exercise similar courage and self-discipline in the pursuit of our supreme good, moral wisdom.

Elsewhere, Marcus argues that the Stoic art of life is more like the wrestler's than the dancer's — and he had ample experience of both disciplines. In life we must learn to stand firm, like a wrestler, and be ready to meet the attacks of fortune, which may be sudden and unexpected.[8] He also reflects on the way "pleasant song and dance" can lose its charm if we "separate the melody of the voice into its individual sounds," and suggests that we can do the same watching a dance by thinking of it as broken up into individual movements.[9] This is an astute psychological observation, which he applies to life in general by thinking of challenging experiences as if they were divided into smaller chunks, easier to manage and less overwhelming emotionally. Such passages are typical of the way Marcus used imagery from his everyday experiences to express his Stoic philosophy of life.

The honors that the emperor heaped upon Marcus as a child suggest he was already preparing him to be a potential successor, albeit alongside other candidates. Hadrian clearly admired the boy, and the two had much in common. Their families both came from

Andalusia, in southern Spain. They had both lost their fathers at an early age – indeed, Hadrian's parents died when he was ten. Hadrian was, moreover, famous for being, like Marcus's mother, a Hellenophile. He was the first Roman emperor to sport a full beard, with the result that his profile on coins made him appear Grecianized and hinted at his intellectual pretensions. Marcus, who barely left Rome as a child, except perhaps for brief holidays in the Italian countryside, must have fantasized about accompanying the emperor on his trips to distant Athens.

Hadrian had been nicknamed the "Little Greek" in his youth, and he enthusiastically embraced the Greek Sophist movement. He erected a center for learning called the Athenaeum, in honor of Athens, near the Capitoline Hill in Rome. The emperor's favorite Greek orator was Favorinus of Arelate (modern-day Arles, France). Favorinus was an intersex individual, born with male genitals but no testicles, and reputedly possessing a mixture of other male and female characteristics. He taught both Greek rhetoric and the philosophy of Academic Skepticism, derived from Plato's school, which maintained that certainty is impossible although some thoughts may be more plausible than others. Favorinus was also the friend and teacher of two men, Herodes Atticus and Alexander Peloplaton, who would later become tutors to Marcus Aurelius.

Hadrian, who wanted to be a writer and orator himself, vied with the Sophists for public acclaim. "And although he was very deft at prose and at verse and very accomplished in all the arts, yet he used to subject the teachers of these arts, as though more learned than they, to ridicule, scorn, and humiliation. With these very professors and philosophers he often debated by means of pamphlets or poems issued by both sides in turn." On one occasion, the emperor petulantly insisted that Favorinus was using a word incorrectly even though the usage was derived from several reputable authors. Favorinus yielded, despite knowing that Hadrian was wrong. When others complained that he should not have backed down, the Sophist quipped, "You are urging a wrong course, my friends, when you do not suffer me to regard as the most learned of men the one who has thirty legions." Eventually, after crossing swords once too often with Hadrian, Favorinus appears to have been exiled and was grateful, he claimed, to have escaped with his life.[10] As in Hans Christian Andersen's "The Emperor's New Clothes," few remaining at court had the courage to tell Emperor Hadrian when he was making himself appear foolish.

Marcus, like his mother, preferred more down-to-earth and plainspoken company. While staying at the villa of his grandfather, for example, Marcus was in the care of a male childminder and tutor (*tropheus*). Private tutoring was part of the primary education of upper-class Roman boys, and it usually began around age seven. Marcus's tutor was most likely a slave or freedman, perhaps of Greek origin, living in Annius Verus's household. Marcus would have been in the same man's care for years, playing children's games and learning to read and write each day under his tutor's watchful eye.

Among those whose virtues Marcus listed in the *Meditations*, this slave is the only one left anonymous.[11] Yet even as emperor, four decades later, he still recalled the profound impression the man made upon him. By contrast, Herodes Atticus, who was not only the most acclaimed orator in the empire but also Marcus's Greek rhetoric master and an old family friend, goes completely unmentioned and uncredited. Instead, the author of the *Meditations* heaps praise on his nameless childhood tutor, placing him on an equal footing with the great Roman statesmen and celebrated Greek intellectuals who shaped his character.

Marcus's tropheus taught him to avoid getting carried away at spectator sports or, as he put it, to take sides with neither the Small

Shields (Thracians) nor the Large Shields (Samnites) in the gladiatorial games. Neither was he to prefer the Green or the Blue team at the chariot racing. I think Marcus interpreted these words to mean that one should avoid taking sides wherever possible in life and treat partisan individuals with caution. When, as emperor, encamped on the Danube frontier, he finally wrote down this childhood advice, Marcus was more concerned with warring tribes and political factions than with the supporters of opposing chariot teams.

The same childhood tutor also taught Marcus to work with his hands and to endure hardship, and showed him how to be content when his basic needs were met. He advised the young boy never to meddle in other people's business, and to turn a deaf ear to slander. This humble, anonymous tutor was everything Hadrian and the Sophists were not. Lucilla, who shared some values with her son's tropheus, probably appointed him for that reason. Marcus admired the down-to-earth, honest character exhibited both by his mother and by his tropheus. In his notes, the simple virtues that Marcus learned early in life from his family and childminder come before any explicit mention of philosophy. He lists them at the start of the *Meditations,* as if they provided the foundation upon which his subsequent education in Stoic philosophy would be built.

Even as a young boy, Marcus struck those who met him as a future philosopher. The *Augustan History* states that some time after the death of Marcus's father, Hadrian started calling the child *Verissimus.*[12] The emperor had chosen Marcus as a potential successor because the boy was a relative of a suitable age, who was "already giving indication of exceptional strength of character," qualities that reputedly earned him the nickname.[13] Marcus's family name Verus can mean "True." Hadrian's joke was that the boy's name should be elevated to *Verissimus,* "Most True" or "Truest," as if to say that he was the most honest and plainspoken person in Rome.

Truthfulness was a virtue extolled by Marcus throughout his life. "Speak both in the senate and to every man, whoever he may be, appropriately, not with any affectation," he later wrote in the *Meditations,* adding, "Use plain discourse."[14] It sounds almost as if Marcus, like the little boy in "The Emperor's New Clothes," may have blurted out some awkward truth that the rest of the court was afraid to voice. The historians do not tell us what he said to the emperor to earn his nickname, but it stuck and became common knowledge. Roughly three decades later, for instance, Marcus was addressed as "Verissimus the Philosopher" by the Christian apologist Justin Martyr.[15]

Indeed, Marcus appeared to be an unusually serious child from his earliest years.[16] He would learn in due course from his philosophy tutors about the Cynic-Stoic tradition of *parrhesia,* "plain speaking" or frankness. In early childhood, though, the individual most responsible for encouraging young Verissimus to be remarkably honest was his mother, the woman known for detesting those who hid one thing in their hearts while their lips spoke another.

At some point, Lucilla left her father-in-law's villa and returned to her own home nearby on the Caelian Hill, taking her son with her. Marcus, it appears, was glad to leave when he did and, looking back, he thanked the gods "that I was not brought up with my grandfather's concubine any longer than I was, and that I preserved the flower of my youth, and that I did not prove my virility before the proper age, but even deferred the time."[17]

Was their departure due to problems caused by the old man's lover? This passage might be implying that she made sexual advances toward the boy, although Marcus was probably no older than twelve at the time. Whatever the meaning, one gets the impression that young Marcus became troubled, and he and Lucilla may have left under something of a cloud. Once again, looking back, Marcus would refer to this move as nothing to be feared, despite comparing it to a death of sorts.

Traditionally, it was the responsibility of Roman matriarchs to oversee the education of their children, an arrangement that gave women a degree of behind-the-scenes influence in Roman society. Lucilla was an exceptionally erudite woman, an intellectual. She was still a young widow, and she had pointedly taken her son back under her own roof, thereby affirming her autonomy and her control over his upbringing. The choice of Marcus's tutors at this time in particular reflects his mother's values, and her side of the family were prepared to pay generously for his education: "As soon as he passed beyond the age when children are brought up under the care of nurses, he was handed over to advanced instructors and attained a knowledge of philosophy."[18] Private tuition from expensive foreign teachers became an important feature of Marcus's life after he turned twelve and left behind his old tropheus. It was at this remarkably young age that he would first become interested in philosophy.

CHAPTER THREE

The Greek Training

One morning Marcus Aurelius's favorite tutor took him to join a group of older boys as they crammed into a busy school hall, writing tablets dangling from their necks. Marcus was the only one still wearing the golden bulla (protective amulet) that marked him as a child. He must have been thrilled to witness something normally reserved for those who had donned the *toga virilis* and legally achieved manhood. The boys were crowded around a foreign lecturer, who was dressed in a simple gray shawl, with long white hair and a well-kempt beard that added to his sagelike appearance. He spoke eloquently in Greek, the language of philosophy, often stopping to answer questions from excited students. Originally from Asia Minor, Apollonius of Chalcedon had recently been teaching Stoicism in Athens, but now he was the talk of Rome.

Apollonius would have given speeches exhorting Roman youths to study philosophy. He doubtless told them the fable known today as the Choice of Hercules. Nearly five centuries earlier, this tale had inspired Zeno, the founder of the Stoic school, to dedicate his life to philosophy. We can imagine Marcus listening transfixed to the story of how the young Heracles (as Hercules was known to the Greeks) lost his way and was forced to choose between two diverging paths, a decision that would shape his character for the rest of his life. On one side lay pleasure and vice, on the other discipline and virtue. The goddess of virtue, Arete, appeared to Heracles, giving a compelling argument for choosing the harder of the two paths. The moral was clear: although a life of pleasure might seem appealing, true fulfillment comes only by following the path of virtue. In his early teens, Marcus would have heard other such exhortations, which inspired young men to dream of becoming philosophers.

Philosophy was, nevertheless, an advanced academic subject, one that only a fraction of Marcus's childhood companions studied in depth. They would usually begin the course after reaching the age of fifteen, so long as they made good initial progress in their study of rhetoric. Greek-speaking tutors, in particular, who traveled to Rome from Athens, Egypt, or Asia Minor, could command high fees. The salaries quoted, for instance, by Philostratus in his *Lives of the Sophists* vary from tens of thousands to hundreds of thousands of Greek drachmas. It would take the average skilled worker many decades to earn what a leading Sophist might charge for a single speech. Although we might expect the Stoics to have charged less than the Sophists, as they typically condemned love of wealth as a vice, Apollonius had a reputation for expecting to be paid very generously.[1]

Marcus's mother had invested in a program of education for her son that was not only unusually costly but covered topics far ahead of his years. Few Roman twelve-year-olds received home tuition from "advanced instructors" on the finer points of Greek philosophy. At this stage of his secondary education, it fell to Marcus's grammarians to give him a head start on topics usually reserved for older boys doing their tertiary studies. Remarkably, it was the painting master appointed by Lucilla, a Greek named Diognetus, who first acquainted Marcus with philosophy and accompanied the boy to several public lectures.[2] Diognetus also had young Marcus try his hand at writing dialogues, doubtless of a philosophical nature.

Marcus attributes several moral lessons to Diognetus.[3] The painting master taught him not to preoccupy himself with trifling amusements, such as the popular Roman sport of quail fighting, and perhaps cautioned him against gambling in general. He also convinced Marcus to view with skepticism self-proclaimed miracle workers, sorcerers, and exorcists. (The latter was apparently a reference to early Christians, still viewed as superstitious fanatics by many Romans.) Similar reminders to maintain focus on the true goal of philosophy and not be distracted by trivial pursuits or lose himself down intellectual rabbit holes would later become a theme of the *Meditations*. In the midst of this moral education, ironically, we find no mention of the painting master having taught Marcus anything about *painting* — presumably they were too busy strolling around Lucilla's gardens talking and sharing their mutual love of philosophy.

Diognetus also taught Marcus to be tolerant of plain speaking, a concept associated with several schools of philosophy. The Cynics, however, were especially known for this virtue. Diognetus most likely exhibited similar frankness, a trait highly regarded by Marcus's mother, as we have seen. Now, though, the little boy whom Hadrian had dubbed Verissimus for his outspokenness had to learn to be gracious when he found himself on the receiving end of unvarnished remarks from his tutors.

It was also the painting master who taught Marcus to desire "a straw camp-bed and animal pelt, and whatever else of the kind belongs to the Greek training" (*Ellenike agoge*).[4] Marcus's use of this phrase is striking because the word *agoge* is best known as a reference to military cadet training of the kind young boys were put through in Sparta. For certain philosophers, military traditions such as sleeping on a straw mat, wearing a rough woolen cloak, and undergoing other, similar hardships formed part of a larger program of self-improvement training. Despite his already wanting to be a philosopher at the age of twelve and attending some lectures, one suspects Marcus was not yet able to fully immerse himself in the scholarly aspects of the subject. So he began by copying the outward *behavior* of certain philosophers, such as their plain speaking, rudimentary attire, and ascetic practices.

Even Lucilla, praised by Marcus for her "simple" way of life (at least compared to other wealthy Romans), clearly found his behavior odd at times: "He studied philosophy with ardor, even as a youth. For when he was twelve years old he adopted the dress and, a little later, the hardiness of a philosopher, pursuing his studies clad in a rough Greek cloak and sleeping on the ground; at his mother's solicitation, however, he reluctantly consented to sleep on a couch strewn with skins."[5] What the historian means by "rough Greek cloak" is the traditional philosopher's shawl or *tribon,* a cheap garment made from coarse gray wool. The more austere sects wore this without a tunic (*chiton*) underneath, often with one shoulder left bare — a way of dressing dubbed "semi-naked" by Greeks and Romans. For a precocious young Roman of Marcus's station to dress and act like an ascetic beggar-philosopher must have seemed like an affectation, even to cultured individuals such as his mother.

The embrace of voluntary hardship — wearing crude attire, going barefoot, sleeping on a straw mat on the ground — was mostly associated with Cynic philosophy, from which Stoicism in part derived. Marcus alludes to Cynicism several times in the *Meditations.* He seems, for instance, to have Cynics in mind when he writes, "The one is a philosopher without a tunic, and the other without a book: here is another half naked. 'Bread I have not,' he says, 'and I abide by reason – and I do not get the means of living out of my learning, and I abide by my reason.'"[6] In addition to going about half-naked and sneering at bookish learning, Cynics also tended to earn no money from their teaching, preferring instead to beg for their daily bread. Although Marcus always respected the Cynics, he eventually came to prefer the more urbane Stoic school. One reason was that the Cynics emphasized indifference toward external things, including other people. The Stoics adopted this notion of indifference (*apatheia*) but in a milder form, placing more emphasis on the value of healthy emotions, particularly love or natural affection.

Although love of philosophy replaced sports and other common pursuits, leaving Marcus increasingly "serious and dignified," the *Augustan History* notes that it did not take away from the geniality, or natural affection, he continued to show toward his household, friends, and casual acquaintances. His character was well-balanced: "austere, though not unreasonable, modest, though not inactive, and serious without gloom."[7] He was also "named and beloved variously as brother, father, or son by various men," according to their age.[8] In short, although he was maturing into a grave young man, committed to the study of an austere philosophy, Marcus continued to be known for his warmth, friendship, and affection.

Today many people assume that the Stoics were cold and *unemotional*. That is typically because they confuse "Stoicism" (capitalized), the Greek philosophy, with stoicism (lowercase), the "stiff upper-lip" style of coping with adversity. Although this is a fundamental misinterpretation, the image of Stoicism as a cold and dispassionate philosophy is found even in ancient sources. Marcus's family friend, the Sophist Herodes Atticus, was critical of the Stoics for precisely this reason. He compares them to an uneducated man who cuts down all the crops in his field along with the weeds, or, as we might say today, like someone who "throws the baby out with the bathwater": "Thus it is that those disciples of insensibility, wishing to be thought calm, courageous and steadfast because of showing neither desire nor grief, neither wrath nor joy, root out all the more vigorous emotions of the mind, and grow old in the torpor of a sluggish and, as it were, nerveless life."[9] Marcus was not swayed by criticisms such as these. Whereas Herodes was notorious for his violent temper, Marcus found the Stoics admirable both for their equanimity and their natural affection. One of his favorite Stoic tutors "never showed anger or any other passion," for instance, but was "entirely free from passion and yet full of natural affection."[10]

Indeed, the Stoic ideal was to be free of irrational and unhealthy passions and yet full of rational and healthy ones, particularly natural affection. Commendable emotions such as friendship and love play an important role in the philosophy. For the Stoics, to love someone is to wish for that person to flourish, so long as nothing prevents this — to hope, in other words, that the loved one may acquire virtue. We could say, then, that Stoicism tried to marry love with wisdom. Indeed, the purest form of love is the desire to attain wisdom and share it with others for the common good.

The very quality that Fronto had found most lacking among patricians was therefore exemplified by the Stoic teachers, whom Marcus was just beginning to encounter. He first witnessed this quality, however, in his mother.[11] The values that Marcus inherited from his family — moral integrity, humility, freedom from anger, kindness, honesty — made him a natural Stoic. The tutors later appointed to train him in Stoicism would nurture and reinforce precisely these traits.

Many individuals have turned to philosophy, indeed, not because it promised wisdom, but because it promised freedom from distress, or the ability to foster what we today call "emotional resilience." Marcus in the *Meditations* described his childhood as consisting of many losses and changes. Looking back, he asked himself: "Is this anything to fear ?"[12] The repeated upending of a young boy's life would inevitably make him feel quite anxious. His mother's presence alone remained constant. Lucilla was always there for him. At least that is the impression we get, especially from the letters of Fronto. As Marcus found himself drawn ever closer to the rarefied atmosphere of the imperial court, he looked to the friendship of his tutors and love of his family to keep him grounded and give him a sense of perspective on events. Such an attitude would be much needed as the political climate at Rome grew increasingly unpredictable and fraught with danger once the emperor, Hadrian, finally returned from his travels.

CHAPTER FOUR

Hadrian's Vendettas

In 123, during his first tour of the empire, Hadrian visited the city of Claudiopolis in the Roman province of Bithynia (modern-day northwest Turkey). It was probably on this trip that a twelve-year-old local boy named Antinous caught the emperor's eye. A few years later, Hadrian returned to Rome with him, around the time the emperor gave Marcus the nickname Verissimus. Because of his closeness to the emperor, the four- or five-year-old Marcus must have grown increasingly aware of this older boy, known for his exceptional beauty and charisma, who was rapidly becoming a prominent member of the imperial retinue. As both youths were favorites of Hadrian, they certainly knew of and probably even rubbed shoulders with one another. Yet although Antinous was one of the most famed individuals of the era, Marcus makes no mention of him whatsoever, perhaps pointedly. Around 128, Hadrian left for a second time, touring Greece, Asia Minor, and North Africa, with Antinous accompanying him. Marcus remained in Rome with his family.

Hadrian's relationship with Antinous was portrayed as an instance of Greek *paiderastia*, the love of an adolescent boy by an older man. This was not always a sexual relationship, although it seems to have been so in the case of Hadrian and Antinous. One ancient historian claims that, around this time, "malicious rumors" had already begun spreading through Rome that Hadrian had "debauched young men and that he burned with passion for the scandalous attentions of Antinous." He concludes that the nature of the relationship between Hadrian and Antinous was uncertain, although the emperor's reputation for sexual indulgence made people "suspicious of a relationship between men far apart in age."[1] These suspicions appear widespread enough that we must imagine them to have reached the ears of Marcus's family.

Such gossip was fueled by the circulation of erotic verses about Antinous, penned by the emperor himself, and perhaps by his autobiographical account of their relationship, although neither survives today. Hadrian reportedly composed many poems about his lovers, works that revealed a man driven "to excess in the gratification of his desires."[2] Some of these are described as love poems but many were somewhat coarse in nature. The satirist Apuleius, for one, admits to having read many lewd (*lascivus*) poems by Hadrian.[3]

Paiderastia had been an accepted aspect of Greek sexual mores for centuries. Many Romans considered it acceptable as long as the passive partner, the youth, was not a Roman citizen or a freeborn subject, like Antinous, but rather a "barbarian" or a slave. Even so, it was far from being uncontroversial. Marcus later applauds his adoptive father Antoninus Pius for putting an end to "all erotic love for boys," which seems to be a condemnation of pederasty.[4]

In August 130, Hadrian and Antinous arrived at Alexandria, where they visited the tomb of Alexander the Great. There was unease and gossip among the Alexandrian elite about Hadrian's sexual activities, particularly those involving Antinous. As the youth approached his late teens and began to grow a beard, it would have been considered increasingly degrading for him to continue in the role of passive sexual partner.[5]

Hadrian traveled to nearby Libya to hunt a big cat known as the Marousian Lion, which had been troubling the locals. According to a poem by Pancrates, Hadrian deliberately wounded the lion without slaying it in order to give Antinous the opportunity to claim the kill. However, the enraged lion lunged at them.[6] Hadrian saved Antinous, slaying the beast by his own hand. The emperor turned this story into a piece of propaganda celebrating his heroism, which he spread far and wide.

A few weeks later, during a cruise up the Nile, the nineteen-year-old Antinous was found dead. Hadrian wept "like a woman" over his lover's corpse.[7] The incident was perceived by many as suspicious. Some claimed that Antinous had voluntarily sacrificed himself in an exotic ritual — "it being necessary that a life should be surrendered freely for the accomplishment of the ends Hadrian had in view." Hadrian's autobiographical account, by contrast, claimed that the Bithynian youth had simply "fallen in the Nile" and drowned.[8] Another source attributes Antinous's death, somewhat cryptically, to "what both his beauty and Hadrian's sensuality suggest."[9] His fate remains one of the great enigmas of Roman history.

Following Antinous's untimely death, Hadrian had the youth deified, a controversial measure pushed through without Senate approval. The emperor built temples around the world housing sacred statues of Antinous and founded a new cult devoted to the worship of his dead lover, with annual games and festivals in his honor. Some ridiculed the Antinous religion as superstitious nonsense or scorned it as shameless fraud. It was even said to be common knowledge that the oracles pronounced from its temples were composed by Hadrian himself.[10] Marcus probably shared these misgivings as, despite his fascination with religion, this was one cult in which he showed no interest.

The emperor continued his travels for several years, but illness eventually forced his return to Rome in 133, when Marcus was twelve. From this point on, young Verissimus's life became thoroughly entwined with the drama surrounding the imperial court, for not everyone welcomed Hadrian's return. Although the emperor was popular with ordinary people, having improved their lives in many ways, as his health deteriorated he grew increasingly paranoid, violent, and despotic. Marcus witnessed this decline at close quarters over the next four years. The Hadrian he knew throughout this final stage of his life was a brokenhearted, physically and mentally ill man. With tensions mounting in Rome, Marcus came to realize that his being groomed by Hadrian as a potential heir placed him personally, as well as those close to him, in grave danger.

Hadrian's character had always been mercurial: "stern and genial, somber and lewd, hesitant and hurrying, tight-fisted and generous, deceitful and straightforward, cruel and merciful."[11] One critic put this down to good old-fashioned duplicity: "He adroitly concealed a mind envious, melancholy, hedonistic, and excessive with respect to his own ostentation; he simulated restraint, affability, clemency, and conversely disguised the ardor for fame with which he burned."[12] Another historian offers the same explanation: Hadrian put on phony displays of kindness and generosity for a time to cover up his natural cruelty.[13] He was terrified of sharing the same fate as Emperor Domitian, who was assassinated and posthumously vilified as a tyrant. Although it was standard for Roman emperors to be deified after their death, the Senate refused to do so for Domitian, instead imposing a *damnatio memoriae*, eradicating his name from history. Hadrian would avoid a similar fate by a hair's breadth.

Hadrian's accession to the throne in 117 had been mired in controversy. His Praetorian prefect had immediately ordered four of the new emperor's opponents, all men of consular rank, summarily executed. Hadrian denied responsibility and tried to reassure the Senate by swearing an oath never to take any of its members' lives. As the beginning of his rule was stained with blood, however, the Senate felt sure that Hadrian's tyrannical streak was only in temporary abeyance. If he did not get his way, he was bound, sooner or later, to resort again to violence. For much of his rule he had stayed out of trouble simply by staying away from Rome. Now he was back in the city, nearing the end of life, and the indecisive, petty, deceitful, and cruel side of Hadrian's nature came to the fore once again. When Marcus later bemoaned the vicious nature of court life, he surely recalled this, the most turbulent political period he ever witnessed at Rome.

Many years later, one of the era's finest Greek orators, Aelius Aristides, composed a speech praising an emperor, believed to be Antoninus Pius. Aristides, who was born in the year Hadrian came to power, dwells on the favorable contrast between Antoninus's rule and that of his predecessors.[14] The subtext has not escaped modern scholars: "What is remarkable . . . is what Aristides appears to say obliquely about Hadrian: his immorality, meddlesomeness, and caprice, his secret agents, the burdens imposed by his rule, his jealousy of Greek literati, his execution of eminent senators." Marcus was most likely among the audience for Aristides' speech, which captures the bitter resentment of Rome's elite for the unjust and violent way in which Hadrian took the throne. Certain emperors, the orator pointed out, committed "murders, destroying many of those in high position," which meant the legit-imacy of their rule was left in question.[15] Such rulers feared that senior statesmen were conspiring against them, and tarnished their reputations by exiling or executing their perceived enemies. These digs would be aimed at Hadrian by future generations.

Two decades into his rule, the emperor's growing alienation from powerful factions within Rome's ruling elite was already near-ing a crisis, into which young Marcus found himself drawn. Hadrian spent most of his time at his villa in Tibur (modern-day Tivoli), on the edge of the Sabine hills, about twenty miles east of Rome. This vast complex is estimated to have spanned almost three hun-dred acres and contained more than thirty buildings. Although known in some ways for having the common touch, Hadrian now lived in opulent luxury, like a decadent monarch. Guests were waited upon by hundreds of slaves and freedmen, many of whom occupied dingy, smoke-filled subterranean dwellings connected by tunnels. At the center, the sickly emperor had built a round dwell-ing on an island surrounded by a moat with removable wooden bridges where he could isolate himself completely and retreat from his own guests and courtiers.

Throughout Hadrian's final years, the orator Fronto continued to heap praise on him before the Senate in widely read speeches. Years later, he would try to downplay those panegyrics, telling Marcus that he spoke only out of a sense of duty, not real affection. Whereas Lucilla reminded Fronto of the goddess Athena, he saw Hadrian in a very different light: "I wished to appease and propi-tiate Hadrian, as I might Mars Gradivus or Father Dis, rather than loved him."[16] So besides the personification of legions grimly march-ing into battle, Hadrian also reminded Fronto of Dis, or Hades, the dark tyrannical ruler of the underworld. These were gods that one *feared* rather than loved. Fronto would insist to Marcus that he had no choice but to praise Hadrian even though in reality he found the man both menacing and pretentious.

Once Hadrian's health began to fail, the emperor occupied himself with plans for his own funeral. As the vaults of Augustus were full, he started building a grand mausoleum on the banks of the Tiber (now the Castel Sant'Angelo), where his remains would be interred. He became obsessed with the memory of Antinous, his dead lover, and the prospect of his own demise. Cooped up in a grotesquely opulent palace complex of his own design, slowly dying, the emperor descended into a bunker mentality that marred the end of his reign. Young Marcus observed his deterioration with growing unease.

In March 136, as he approached the age of fifteen, Marcus became an adult under Roman law and donned the toga virilis. Hadrian already had plans for his Verissimus, and he immediately betrothed Marcus to a young girl named Ceionia Fabia, the daughter of a patrician called Lucius Ceionius Commodus.[17] Soon after this, Marcus was made prefect of the city for the Latin Festival. This was a ceremonial role, although it served as an opportunity for Marcus to appear and perhaps speak in public. He made a lasting impression on both the senators and the imperial court.[18] This fatherless young man was rapidly gaining the attention, and the respect, of Roman society.

In Hadrian's final years, the emperor began to regard almost all of his former friends as enemies. He attacked his Greek secretary, an Epicurean philosopher called Avidius Heliodorus, "in a most slanderous pamphlet" and apparently stripped him of his position.[19] Other prominent statesmen were reduced to poverty or forced to commit suicide.[20] From the beginning of his rule, Hadrian had become notorious for vendettas against intellectuals who crossed swords with him. The great architect Apollodorus of

Damascus made the mistake of sneering at Hadrian's pretensions and was sent into exile, where he died.[21] The Sophists Favorinus of Arelate and Dionysius of Miletus were lucky to evade a similar fate. Hadrian sought to have them executed but could "find no plausible pretext" for doing so.[22] Favorinus later boasted of the "paradox" that he had disputed with Hadrian and lived. The emperor attacked not only prominent intellectuals and statesmen but also lowly freedmen and soldiers who had no means to defend themselves. His greatest wrath, however, was reserved for those closest to him in power.

Whereas young Marcus had learned to turn a deaf ear to slander, Hadrian's philosophy was quite the opposite: he pried into everything. "Every subject had been cowed and enslaved by fear," it was said, "since many spies went around eavesdropping in every city for anything a person might utter."[23] In fact, many Roman emperors, including Hadrian, relied on *delatores*, hired informers, who were generously rewarded with a share of the accused's wealth for bringing allegations against those suspected of treason. Marcus had grown up under the gaze of this oppressive political regime.

From early in his rule, Hadrian had also assigned military spies known as the *frumentarii* to gather information on his enemies throughout the empire. As the emperor came to rely upon this network of agents in order to retain his grip on power, they began to function more like the secret police of a totalitarian state.[24] Warnings circulated, for instance, that the frumentarii sometimes resorted to entrapment: "In this way also the incautious are caught by the soldiers at Rome. A soldier sits by you in a common dress and begins to speak ill of [the emperor]; then you, as if you had received a pledge of his fidelity by his having begun the abuse, utter yourself also what you think, and then you are carried off in chains."[25] Romans needed to bear in mind that anything said to others could be reported to the authorities. Then again, it was joked, if the emperor executed everyone who abused him verbally, he would have nobody left over whom to rule.[26]

If this much was common knowledge, Marcus and his family must also have known that Hadrian's network of spies and informers engaged in surveillance by intercepting the private letters of his acquaintances. He "pried into all their secrets" so skillfully that those under scrutiny were often surprised to discover how much the emperor knew of their lives. "The wife of a certain man wrote to her husband, complaining that he was so preoccupied by pleasures and baths that he would not return home to her, and Hadrian found this out through his private agents [frumentarii]. And so, when the husband asked for a furlough, Hadrian reproached him with his fondness for his baths and his pleasures. Whereupon the man exclaimed: 'What, did my wife write you exactly what she wrote to me?'"[27] The emperor spied in particular upon his own household and those of his friends.[28] We can assume that he had planted spies in the households of his prospective successors, including that of young Marcus's family. When it is reported, therefore, that Marcus was "reared in Hadrian's lap" this surely meant *under his scrutiny*.[29]

Given the threat of execution merely for speaking ill of one's emperor in private, Lucilla's advice to her son to purge even his *mind* of wrongdoing sounds like a basic condition of survival. Marcus had to learn to control his tongue by controlling his innermost thoughts. He would later write that he aspired to do nothing for which walls or curtains were required.[30] These words take on a sinister meaning when we realize they came from someone who grew up in a regime in which informers, even in his own home, could be opening his letters, and watching his every move.

Hadrian worried more and more about the succession. He had

been prone to nosebleeds, which now became so copious that he feared for his life. Later that year, "when he was burdened by old age and weakened by cruel disease," he made the surprising decision to adopt Marcus's prospective father-in-law, Lucius Ceionius Commodus, naming him as his successor.[31] The *Augustan History* says bluntly that this was "against the wishes of everyone."[32] Apart from being the son of a former consul, Ceionius Commodus had little to his credit. Nevertheless, the emperor loved him, granting him more influence at court than anyone had had since Antinous. Some insinuated that he too had been Hadrian's lover and that his "sole recommendation" was his physical beauty.[33] Ceionius Commodus suffered from his own chronic health problems, though, and frequently vomited blood. Marcus thus found himself betrothed to the daughter of a sickly man earmarked to become the next emperor.

Hadrian then renamed Lucius Ceionius Commodus as "Lucius Aelius Caesar" and elevated him to the office of consul. By Hadrian's time, "Caesar," originally the cognomen of Julius Caesar, had become a conventional title designating the official heir to the throne.[34] Following this, Hadrian put on games at the Circus Maximus in honor of his chosen successor, buying the support of both the people and the army by granting them a donative of four hundred million sesterces. This huge sum was equal to roughly two years' pay for every Roman legionary. The new Caesar's health had deteriorated so badly, however, that he was unable to deliver a speech to the Senate thanking his adoptive father, the emperor.

As a result, Rome became anxious that Hadrian's ill-conceived plans would lead them into a succession crisis. Soon the emperor began admitting that by designating this Lucius as his heir he was leaning against a "tottering wall" and grumbled to his intimates that the vast financial gift bestowed upon the new Caesar had been wasted.[35] Hadrian, in despair, began muttering to his friends melancholy lines from Vergil's *Aeneid:*

> This youth (the blissful vision of a day)
> Shall just be shown on earth, and snatch'd away.[36]

When Lucius Aelius Caesar heard rumors that the emperor expected him to die soon and was talking in private about replacing him, he became consumed with anxiety. (Perhaps he worried he might end up at the bottom of a river like Antinous!)

Around this time, in 135, Marcus's great-aunt, the Empress Vibia Sabina, suddenly passed away. Over the course of a long and childless marriage, Hadrian and Sabina had become estranged from, and even grew to hate, each other. Early in his rule, informers planted in the imperial household reported that many of the emperor's own acquaintances had been behaving toward his wife "in a more familiar manner than the etiquette of the court demanded," insinuating romantic or possibly sexual liaisons.[37] The men he dismissed included his Praetorian prefect and an imperial secretary named Suetonius Tranquillus, famous to later generations as the author of *The Twelve Caesars*. Hadrian often said that he would have divorced his wife, "on the grounds of ill-temper and irritability," had she not already been proclaimed empress.[38]

Sabina, it was claimed, despised her husband as a monster and "had taken pains lest, to the bane of the human race, she become pregnant by him."[39] As her death occurred at the time when Hadrian's behavior was descending into tyranny and violence, foul play was inevitably suspected. "He put many others to death, either openly or by treachery, and indeed, when his wife Sabina died, the rumor arose that the Emperor had given her poison."[40] Others claimed that the empress was driven to suicide.[41] The half-sister of

Marcus's grandfather Marcus Annius Verus, Sabina was perhaps the first of his relatives to fall victim to Hadrian's latest wave of purges.

Shortly after his wife's demise, the emperor, now in his sixties, nearly died of a severe hemorrhage. Tortured in private by his long-standing suspicions about his political rivals, Hadrian had reputedly "controlled all the force of his innate cruelty," at least in public, until this particular health scare.[42] He now became furious with the Senate and, fearing a conspiracy to depose him, leveled charges of treason against his sister's husband, the senior statesman Lucius Servianus.

Servianus, in his nineties, had been appointed consul three times, sharing this distinction with his friend and rival Marcus Annius Verus, Marcus's grandfather. A marble tablet found in Rome bears a curious poem written by an unnamed elder statesman, quite possibly Servianus, addressed to the elder Marcus. It celebrates Verus's third consulship and jokes about his skill at "playing with a glass ball" – an appropriate metaphor for the game of politics. At the time, this pair of three-time consuls were the two most senior statesmen in the empire. Their power and influence can only have grown during the extended periods when Hadrian was abroad, leaving the Senate in charge at Rome.

Servianus had once been touted as a potential successor to Hadrian.[43] After Lucius Aelius was named Caesar, though, the elder statesman fell into disfavor. The emperor began to suspect Servianus of being a potential usurper, plotting to become installed as regent while maneuvering for his teenage grandson to take the throne. We are told that Hadrian, like Domitian before him, used to complain, "Unhappy is the lot of emperors, who are never believed when they accuse anyone of pretending to the throne until after they are slain."[44] The emperor seems to have lacked hard evidence for his allegations of high treason (*laesa majestas*), and probably based his charges on testimony received from hired informers, or possibly even through torture, for the Senate was never convinced of Servianus's guilt. The emperor, regardless, ordered the old statesman and his grandson to be beheaded. For Servianus, the glass ball was finally about to shatter.

On receiving the news of his death sentence, Servianus asked for fire to make a small sacrifice. Instead of the customary pledges of allegiance to the emperor, he invoked the following curse upon his head: "That I am guilty of no wrong, ye, O Gods, are well aware; as for Hadrian, this is my only prayer, that he may long for death but be unable to die."[45] This was indeed to be Hadrian's fate. His latest bouts of violence were driven by the torment of his several worsening ailments: "burning and impatient with pain, he destroyed many from the senate."[46] By executing a fifth consul, the emperor had violated the sacred oath he had made to the Senate on his accession never to take the life of a single one of them. It was a return to the political purges that had stained the beginning of his rule. Sabina had been the half-sister of Marcus Aurelius's paternal grandfather. As Hadrian's suspicions continued to eat away at him, paranoia would soon be directed against more of Marcus's relatives.

The following year, Lucius Aelius Caesar, Hadrian's designated successor, was appointed consul for a second time and sent to take command of the legions in Pannonia (modern-day Austria). He was so weak he could barely lift his shield, but he led a moderately successful military campaign. However, he returned to Rome more ill than when he left and died on January 1, 138, after an overdose of his medicine, reputedly by accident although it could conceivably have been murder or even suicide. He left behind him a seven-year-old son, Lucius Ceionius Commodus, better known today as Lucius Verus. Lucius Aelius's death made a mess of Hadrian's succession plans, in a way that would come to shape young Marcus

Aurelius's future. As the legitimate son of a Caesar, albeit one recently deceased, Lucius Verus was arguably next in line to the throne. He would not be able to take power though, until he reached adulthood, still eight years away.

Hadrian gave Lucius Aelius an imperial funeral, ordering colossal statues of him to be set up around the empire and temples dedicated to him in several cities. Although these paled in comparison with the monuments commemorating Antinous, the honors bestowed on the departed Caesar were a reminder of his family's claim to the throne, particularly that of the young son he left behind. Marcus Aurelius now found himself in the uncomfortable position of being drawn closer to the emperor under the shadow of a looming succession crisis. Anxiety in Rome was also mounting because with each passing day Hadrian talked more and more about the prospect of his own death.

CHAPTER FIVE

The Death of Hadrian

On January 23, 138, the day before Hadrian's sixty-second birthday, a madman forced his way into the Senate building raving incoherently about death. It took everyone by surprise, most of all Hadrian, who was left profoundly disturbed by the incident. The notoriously superstitious emperor took it to be a portent of his own imminent demise. A day later, while performing a religious rite, the part of his ceremonial toga covering his head fell back, leaving his graying scalp bare. This was another bad omen: the gods were exposing his vulnerability for all to see. Then a signet ring bearing his image dropped from his emaciated finger. It was as though the aging emperor was falling to pieces in public view.

Hadrian experienced other events as sinister omens. Following the demise of Lucius Aelius Caesar, the emperor was giving a speech to the Senate that included the words "after my son's death," referring to Aelius. Somehow, he misspoke and was heard to say, "after my *own* death."[1] Strange visions began to haunt his sleep, leaving him increasingly unnerved. Once he had boasted to the whole empire of saving Antinous's life by boldly slaying the fabled

Marousian Lion. Now he lay awake at night shaking, having dreamt that he was himself being devoured by a monstrous lion. The hunter in this nightmare had literally become the hunted. Perhaps it symbolized Hadrian's fear, as the question of succession loomed, that a growing band of conspirators was plotting to wrest the throne from him. What devoured Hadrian in the end, however, was not a lion but his own sickness, anger, and despair.

Around this time, Hadrian suffered his most serious bout of illness. Already wasting away from blood loss, he had developed severe swelling in his limbs and a chronic subcutaneous skin disease. He was in a terrible state both physically and mentally—a far cry from what philosophers called a "good death." (The wise man, wrote Marcus Aurelius, "acts no tragic part, does not groan, will need neither solitude nor much company" and, most of all, "will live without either pursuing or flying from death.")[2] Whereas Socrates met his end with perfect equanimity, Hadrian spent his final years pursuing revenge for bitter grievances. This was not the type of ruler Marcus wanted to become, and he resolved to meet his own death with composure when the time arrived. He searched for a better role model and was soon to be provided with one.

Later that same year, prompted by growing concerns over his health, Hadrian adopted another son, a senator in his early fifties called Titus Aurelius Fulvus Boionius Arrius Antoninus, better known today as Antoninus Pius. The *Augustan History*'s description of his character is quite something:

> In personal appearance he was strikingly handsome, in natural talent brilliant, in temperament kindly; he was aristocratic in countenance and calm in nature, a singularly gifted speaker and an elegant scholar, conspicuously thrifty, a conscientious land-holder, gentle, generous, and mindful of others' rights. He possessed all these qualities, more-

over, in the proper mean and without ostentation, and, in fine, was praiseworthy in every way and, in the minds of all good men, well deserving of comparison with Numa Pompilius.[3]

The surviving sculptures of Antoninus confirm that he was a handsome man. The comparison with King Numa was also well made since Antoninus's reign was to be, like Numa's, famously peaceful. In the eyes of many senators, he possessed the ideal qualities of a future emperor.

Although Antoninus had had an illustrious political career and was well known throughout the Italian peninsula for his legal and political acumen, in private life he spent his time quietly managing his estates. He had recently served as proconsul of the province of Asia, a role in which he had excelled and earned acclaim. On returning to Rome, he was made an adviser at court, where he was typically found guiding the troubled Emperor Hadrian toward a more merciful course of action. The Senate must have felt that his were a safe pair of hands in which to entrust the empire.

Antoninus was, moreover, Marcus Aurelius's uncle; he had married Annia Galeria Faustina (Faustina the Elder), Marcus's paternal aunt. She had given birth to two sons and two daughters, but by 138 only one of the daughters still lived. Antoninus was adopted on condition, therefore, that he adopt both Marcus and Lucius, the young boy left fatherless by the death of Lucius Aelius.[4] The two boys were in turn adopted by Hadrian as his grandsons. The *Augustan History*, however, notes that apart from his "kindly character" nothing in young Lucius's nature was "capable of shedding luster on the imperial family."[5] The same history also claims that "Hadrian would have taken [Marcus] for his own successor," if the boy had not been too young at the time.[6] Instead, Antoninus was to serve as an interim ruler.

In 120 Antoninus had been appointed consul alongside Catilius Severus, Marcus's maternal great-grandfather, who may have been something of a father figure to the young boy. Catilius had served twice as consul and been made proconsul (governor) of Africa. He was currently urban prefect, the position previously held by Marcus's paternal grandfather, Marcus Annius Verus. Hadrian, by promoting Catilius to such senior positions, made it clear that he trusted the man and held him in high regard. Yet by 138, he had started accusing him of treason. According to the *Augustan History,* "The adoption of Antoninus was lamented by many at that time, particularly by Catilius Severus, the prefect of the city, who was making plans to secure the throne for himself. When this fact became known, a successor was appointed for him and he was deprived of his office."[7] Hadrian must have uncovered this alleged plot not long after adopting both Antoninus and Marcus. If genuine, it would have posed a threat to all their lives.

Catilius could not have planned to act alone. Indeed, we are told that after these events, he and two other former confidants of the emperor were "persecuted vigorously."[8] The first was the Praetorian prefect, Marcius Turbo, whom the emperor removed from office. The other man named was Ummidius Quadratus, a former proconsul of Africa. He was the father-in-law of Marcus Aurelius's sister. If Hadrian's suspicions had any foundation, the involvement of both the urban prefect and the Praetorian prefect in a conspiracy would mean a powerful faction at the highest level of Roman society opposed his rule.

Hadrian's purges were now affecting Marcus's extended family. He and Lucilla could do nothing but look on as both her grandfather and her son-in-law were condemned as traitors, even though the histories make no mention of hard evidence being presented that substantiated the charges. Indeed, the bloodless nature of the punishment hints that the senators were not convinced they were dealing with a genuine act of treason. Hadrian's actions may have been punishment simply for an unguarded comment, overheard by one of his spies.

The young Marcus must have found these events troubling — As soon as he was placed in line to the throne, at least two of his relatives were accused of plotting treason against the emperor and narrowly avoided being beheaded. Catilius, moreover, was not alone in lamenting Hadrian's latest succession plan. Marcus had his own reservations. When he heard that he had been adopted by the emperor, he did not celebrate but rather felt anxious and repulsed — a classic case of *horror imperii,* "fear of ruling." When members of his mother's household asked what was the matter, Marcus rattled off a litany of evils associated in his mind with donning the imperial purple. Decades later he was still complaining about palace life, quoting Fronto's maxim that political tyranny is steeped in envy, deception, and hypocrisy.[9]

Marcus studied Hadrian's behavior closely, however, and learned his lesson well. One historian attributes this maxim to him: "The ruler who emplants in the hearts of his subjects not fear resulting from cruelty, but love occasioned by kindness, is most likely to complete his reign safely. For it is not those who submit from necessity but those who are persuaded to obedience who continue to serve and to suffer without suspicion and without pretense of flattery."[10] These lines, which offer a sharp contrast to Hadrian's behavior, reflect the desire to govern with kindness rather than anger that we find permeating the *Meditations.* Marcus was on the spot to see precisely what befell rulers when their grip on power relied too much on intimidation.

In 138, in the midst of the purges, Hadrian commanded the sixteen-year-old Marcus to leave his mother's home and take up residence in his private villa at Tibur. Hadrian eked out his final years in this opulent complex, surrounded by dozens of statues of Antinous, whose tragic presence haunted the villa's grounds. Marcus made it clear that he did not want to go and live there. He realized that everyone in Hadrian's household was a potential informer. These spies would report whatever they saw or heard to the emperor, just as those who had denounced Hadrian's wife for her indiscretions had done two decades earlier. Marcus must have observed many other things about Hadrian that unsettled him, from his questionable sexual conduct to his dangerous vendettas against former friends and even relatives. During these days, though, the once outspoken Verissimus must have found it hard to speak his mind regarding the emperor.

Hadrian presumably told Marcus that moving to the palace was necessary for his safety. After all, the emperor claimed to have uncovered at least two major "conspiracies" – and a threat to Hadrian was also a threat to his chosen successors. Sidelined contenders for the throne were marked men, and often did not live long. Although still an adolescent, Marcus had been placed in line for the succession. He was being dragged unwillingly into a political crisis where the stakes were life or death.

The night he received the news of his adoption, Marcus had a vivid dream in which he discovered that his arms and shoulders were made of ivory. Worried that they might have lost their strength, he attempted to lift a heavy object. However, to his great surprise, his arms proved even stronger than before. Neither of the two ancient sources that mention this dream offers an interpretation of its meaning.[11] Perhaps it was a symptom of Marcus's anxiety about the prospect of becoming emperor. Yet this strange vision inspired him to feel more confident about his future role. One thing is clear: what appeared at first to be a weakness in the dream turned out to be a strength.

As with all dreams, many different interpretations are possible. I believe, though, that the arms of ivory symbolize the training in Stoic philosophy that Marcus was receiving in his mother's household. Epictetus, for example, often used the strong shoulders of athletes, such as wrestlers in the Olympic games, as a metaphor for philosophy.[12] He exhorted his students to exhibit their Stoic training not by using clever words but through strength of character and virtuous actions. "Do you then show me your improvement in [philosophy]? If I were talking to an athlete, I should say: 'Show me your shoulders!'"[13] In his youth, Marcus saw his role in life as that of a philosopher, not a future emperor, and had no faith that the two could be reconciled. His love of philosophy was considered a weakness — it was more Grecian than Roman and perceived by some as effeminate. (He was later insulted as a "philosophical old woman.")[14] Fortunately, Marcus was about to realize that his training in philosophy could become his greatest asset by preparing him to endure the challenges he would one day have to face.

The emperor, meanwhile, sought to carry on with his purges, ordering that "very many others who were guilty of slight offenses should be put to death."[15] Hadrian had named Antoninus as Caesar immediately after adopting him, though, and awarded him the proconsular and tribunician power. These actions effectively made Antoninus for the last four or five months of Hadrian's life not only his designated successor but also his co-emperor in all but name; he supported the disease-ravaged old man both physically, taking his arm when he walked, and as emperor, as Hadrian's grip on power loosened. Antoninus increasingly had both the personal authority and political powers necessary to intervene and spare the men Hadrian sought to persecute. Marcus was relieved to observe his adoptive father stepping into the breach to moderate his adoptive grandfather's cruelty.

Near the end of his life, in physical agony and consumed by paranoid rage, Hadrian finally despaired. Weakened and tormented by the disease spread throughout his body, he was being "consumed by a miserable death," and frequently begged to be killed.[16] Guided by his physician, he marked a spot on his chest with dye. He then ordered one of his slaves, a Sarmatian huntsman named Mastor, to run him through with a freshly sharpened sword. His suicide plans were leaked to Antoninus, though, who ordered the Praetorian prefects to place Hadrian under guard. Mastor was too afraid to follow his dying master's orders. Ironically, the emperor who had made such controversial use of *delatores* was now denied the freedom to die by an informer in his own house. When Hadrian found out, he lost his temper with the slave who betrayed his trust, and ordered his execution. Once more, Antoninus intervened, this time saving Mastor's life.

Those closest to the emperor, particularly Antoninus and Marcus, continued to watch over him to prevent his suicide.[17] Antoninus, especially, insisted that Hadrian needed to endure his illness, for his suicide would have brought down accusations of murder on those around him. Young Marcus, who still lived under Hadrian's roof, would not have escaped suspicion if the aging emperor had died under mysterious circumstances. The slightest hint of foul play could be used by rival contenders for the throne, and what Rome feared most was another civil war.

Hadrian agreed to draw up a will, although he refused to provide specific instructions for the handover of power. He then tried to kill himself again, with a dagger this time, but it was taken from him. Finally, he ordered his physician to administer poison. The poor man took his own life instead, dreading the consequences for himself and his family if he were accused of murdering the emperor. The prayer of Servianus that Hadrian should long for death but be unable to die was being answered before Marcus's very eyes.

After at least three failed suicide bids, Hadrian retreated to his villa in the luxurious coastal town of Baiae, on the northwest shore of the Bay of Naples. A few generations earlier, Seneca had described it as a pleasure resort brimming with drunken revelers and prostitutes. Baiae was a den of vice, he said, "which the wise man or he who is on the way toward wisdom will avoid as foreign to good morals." Hadrian's last act was to go there.[18]

Meanwhile, Antoninus was left in charge at Rome. When Hadrian's condition finally became critical, he rushed to the emperor's side, just in time to witness his death, on July 10, 138. Hadrian was sixty-two and had ruled Rome for twenty-one years, energetically and conscientiously at first, later through the threat of purges and guided by his insidious web of spies and informers. As he lay dying, surrounded by doctors trying to save his life, he cracked the hackneyed joke: "Many physicians have killed a king!"[19]

The *Augustan History* makes no bones about the fact that Hadrian died "hated by all," which was at least true of the majority of the senatorial class, including prominent members of Marcus's family. "Much was said against him after his death, and by many persons," it adds.[20] Indeed, the senators were so hostile to him that for some time, they tried to annul his acts and deny him the customary honor of deification.[21] Such a refusal would have relegated him to the company of tyrants such as Caligula, Nero, and Domitian for all history.

Antoninus once again intervened, pointing out that repudiating Hadrian's statutes would only create further turmoil. One of Hadrian's acts was to name him Caesar, he said, so they risked casting doubt over the legitimacy of the entire succession, including young

Marcus's claim to throne. The fact that the Senate eventually agreed shows the high regard in which the senators held the new emperor. Whereas Hadrian had used threats of violence to hold on to power, Marcus's adoptive father exerted his influence simply by threatening to resign.

It also speaks to the Senate's terror of another civil war between rival claimants to the throne. The senators would rather go through the motions of honoring Hadrian, whom they considered a tyrant and a monster, than imperil the accession of the new emperor. Things had already started to change now that a man they knew well and trusted, one of their own number, was taking care of the state. We can sense the relief the senators felt when Antoninus finally replaced Hadrian and the threat of political executions ended. Marcus and his family must have shared this sense of relief.

Shortly after Hadrian's death, the Senate awarded Antoninus the cognomen Pius, indicating that he was loyal and dutiful rather than what we mean in English by *pious*. The *Augustan History* recounts multiple reasons for granting this title.[22] One was that Antoninus spared many men who had previously been condemned to death. During his final days, Hadrian had ordered "a large number of the senators, to whom he had been a laughing-stock, to be immediately executed." Antoninus had them held in custody until after the emperor's death and then tactfully argued that Hadrian intended all along to pardon them. The remaining senators were therefore relieved when "those whose death they were grieving suddenly appeared and each one embraced his relatives and friends."[23] A long crisis had ended, and the Senate, in particular, welcomed Antoninus's assurances that there would be no return to such tyranny in the future.

Between the ages of twelve and sixteen, Marcus had a ringside seat from which to observe Hadrian's prolonged illness, and his final descent into despotism and violence. Having been fatherless for over a decade, the young noble was clearly now inspired by the way his adoptive father, Antoninus Pius, handled the crisis. It is as though Marcus had given up hope that a person could live in a palace without being corrupted. Antoninus showed him that it could be done. He had not yet found, however, the shoulders of ivory glimpsed in his dream.

CHAPTER SIX

Disciple of Antoninus

Following Hadrian's death in July 138, Marcus's belongings
were once more packed onto wagons. The young noble was
moving home yet again and embarking on a new life as the adopted
son of the incumbent emperor. Eventually, even his name would
be changed, from Marcus Annius Verus to Marcus Aelius Aurelius
Verus Caesar, affirming the continuity of the dynasties by combin-
ing his own family name with those of Hadrian and Antoninus, the
names Verus, Aelius, and Aurelius, respectively.

Marcus's mother and sister accompanied him to the House of
Tiberius, a mansion on the Palatine Hill named after the emperor
who built it more than a century earlier. Antoninus had relocated
the imperial court from Hadrian's remote villa complex at Tibur
back to the center of Rome. When Marcus and his family arrived,
they must have been confused at first to see palace servants loading
wagons with statues, clothing, and furnishings, as if the emperor
were moving out rather than moving in. On being shown into the
garden, they would have been pleasantly surprised to find Antoninus there dressed in a plain toga, like a private citizen, rather than

imperial robes. His guards had been dismissed; perhaps he was listening intently to one of his servants, discussing the grape harvest at Antoninus's family estate of Lorium, near the coast. The new emperor preferred the simple clothes and bedding made by workers on his own land, which his attendants had shipped to the palace for him.

Marcus soon learned that his adoptive father planned to continue living, as far as possible, as an ordinary citizen, despite his new position. During the course of his rule, Antoninus would reduce imperial pomp to "the utmost simplicity," something which earned him the respect of many people.[1] Yet he was not an ascetic. Although Antoninus was fortunate enough to enjoy a great many advantages in life, he was neither ashamed of them nor took them for granted. He was capable of appreciating the pleasures of imperial life without overindulging in them, and he was never put out if certain luxuries were unavailable. Marcus admired his temperance, and considered this the mark of a man, like Socrates, who had attained a "perfect and invincible soul."[2] That was the ideal shared by Stoic philosophers, who viewed pleasure and the external advantages in life as neither good nor evil. What mattered, Marcus would learn, was to use such things wisely.

Antoninus immediately abolished the use of the hated paid informers and military spies relied upon by his predecessor. As emperor he "freed everyone's spirit" from oppression, it was said, and gave the people back their liberty "whole and entire."[3] This act alone must have transformed the atmosphere throughout the empire, especially in the capital. Rome's powerful families, including Marcus's friends and relatives, could relax and speak more freely, knowing they were no longer under surveillance.

Antoninus was more familiar than Hadrian had been with the other senators, who viewed him as one of their own. They offered him the honorific title Father of the Country (*Pater Patriae*) on his accession. He initially refused it but then accepted a few years later. This title, although conferring no powers, had been introduced by the emperor Augustus, who sought thereby to assume the role of supreme *paterfamilias*, or guardian of the morals of all Roman citizens. Hadrian had waited ten years to receive it, an unusually long time, perhaps reflecting public unease over his suitability to act as a father figure and role model to the nation. Now, though, the empire had a ruler whose morals nobody questioned.

Immediately following Hadrian's death, Antoninus annulled Marcus's engagement to Ceionia Fabia and betrothed him to his own daughter, Faustina the Younger. This confirmed that Marcus, now age seventeen, was next in line to the throne. As Faustina was only seven years old, Marcus would have to wait another seven years until she was considered old enough to marry him. He agreed to the arrangement, although he was hesitant at first and wanted time to think it over. He would later say that he was grateful that he had preserved his virginity for as long as possible, deferring sex until the appropriate age, which the Romans considered to be fifteen, although Marcus claims he waited even longer.[4] Perhaps he even put it off until his wedding night, although that would not be until he was twenty-four. In the same passage, he thanks the gods that he "never touched either Benedicta or Theodotus," a female and male, respectively, perhaps slaves, but otherwise unknown to us.[5] The context seems to make clear that he is referring to sex. It may be that he was tempted by others during his long wait to marry Faustina but restrained himself, albeit with difficulty.

Marcus's first public responsibility as the emperor's son was the organization of an ambitious public funeral, held at Rome, for his adoptive grandfather. Tradition dictated that this should involve a huge gladiatorial tournament, an onerous responsibility for a seventeen-year-old. He did not let the imperial family, or their public, down.

When Marcus turned eighteen he was appointed to the junior office of quaestor. This was the first position in a typical Roman senatorial career, known as the *cursus honorum*, "course of honors." Years earlier, Hadrian had insisted that an exception should be made allowing Marcus to serve in the Senate when he turned eighteen. (His adoptive brother Lucius Verus, by contrast, had to wait until he reached twenty-four, as was the norm.)[6] While some of his peers were sent to serve as military tribunes in the provinces, Marcus was trained to become a career politician. He would serve under Antoninus in the Senate when the latter became consul for the year 139. The same year, Marcus was appointed one of the six commanders of the equestrian order, a quasi-military position, although his duties would have been mainly administrative. Hadrian and Antoninus had agreed, it seems, that Rome would be better ruled by statesmen than soldiers, although Hadrian himself had risen to power through the ranks of the military.

The following year, Marcus had reached only the junior magisterial office of quaestor, yet he was appointed co-consul alongside his adoptive father, who now served his second consulship. Traditionally the honor of a consulship was bestowed on the most experienced senators and restricted to men over the age of forty-two who had reached the preceding rank of praetor, or senior magistrate. Marcus had now attained a higher rank on the cursus honorum than his birth father, Annius Verus. Antoninus also had Marcus inducted into several more of the priestly colleges at the Senate's behest. Today this may seem like nepotism, although it was the norm in Roman society, which assumed that one's closest friends and family usually made the most trustworthy appointees. Antoninus would probably also have argued that Marcus, as Caesar, had to be raised through the ranks as quickly as possible. A decade earlier, Hadrian had caused a succession crisis by naming as Caesar, against everyone's wishes, the undistinguished Lucius Aelius. No questions were raised over Marcus's suitability, though, and the senators wanted everyone to know he had been fully prepared to succeed Antoninus as emperor.

Consequently, Marcus was expected to help Antoninus with his duties, in order to train himself for his future role. Even so, he continued to work at his ongoing, and by now fairly advanced, studies in law, rhetoric, and philosophy. Today we might reasonably describe him as a workaholic. Marcus seems to have been painfully conscious of the responsibilities that accompanied his imperial status. Certainly, his rhetoric tutor Fronto was at times concerned that his student worked too hard, urging him to vacation more and get some rest.

One thing is clear: Marcus saw that his training in Stoic philosophy promised to give him the shoulders of ivory required to endure life at court. He struggled with the impression that hypocrisy, insincerity, and callousness prevailed among Rome's elite.[7] The young Caesar appears to have found refuge in his relationship with his mother, as she differed from most Roman nobles in this regard. "If you had a stepmother and a mother at the same time, you would be dutiful to your stepmother, but still you would constantly return to your mother. Let the court and philosophy now be to you stepmother and mother: return to philosophy frequently and repose in her, through whom what you meet with in the court appears to you tolerable, and you appear tolerable in the court."[8]

"Mother," here, signifies wisdom and philosophy. This must be what Lucilla symbolized for Marcus, like the goddess Athena to whom Fronto compared her. The "stepmother" in this analogy is court life, and of course Marcus's adoptive father's wife was an empress. Empress Faustina the Elder passed away later in the year 140. Although she was a highly esteemed figure in Rome, Marcus says nothing of her unless it is obliquely in this rhetorically brilliant passage. By contrast, Fronto's letters from the period suggest that Marcus and Lucilla remained close. Marcus and Fronto mention Lucilla affectionately many times in their correspondence, but Faustina the Younger, Marcus's betrothed and subsequently his wife, appears, like her mother, only as a vague and peripheral figure. Nevertheless, following Faustina the Elder's demise, Marcus's young wife was about to become the foremost woman in Roman society and throughout the empire.

Antoninus grew fonder of Marcus each day. They were so close, reputedly, that in twenty-three years as father and son, they only parted company for two nights, on two separate occasions.[9] In book 1 of the *Meditations,* Marcus describes the qualities he admires most in others. He lists sixteen individuals in the main section, all of them family members or teachers — his mother is the only woman among them. In addition to these, a concluding passage adds passing mention of Cornificia, his sister; Lucius, his adoptive brother; Faustina, his wife; and their children. Measured simply by the number of words Marcus writes in praise of each of these men and women, it is clear that Antoninus stands head and shoulders above everyone else.[10] Marcus's adoptive father clearly provided him with abundant examples of the virtues taught by Stoicism.

Marcus did not compose his description of Antoninus spontaneously. He lists Antoninus's virtues later in the *Meditations,* describing similar qualities in different words.[11] He has clearly analyzed his character many times. Indeed, Fronto mentions that Marcus often praised the emperor publicly in panegyrics. There is nothing, according to the rhetorician, that his young student could ever say with more honor, truth, and pleasure than what he sets forth in praising his adoptive father.[12] These speeches helped provide the content for a contemplative practice, a sort of Stoic meditation, as Marcus explains in the *Meditations:*

> When you wish to delight yourself, think of the virtues of those who live with you. For instance, the activity of one, and the modesty of another, and the liberality of a third, and some other good quality of a fourth. For nothing delights so much as the examples of the virtues, when they are exhibited in the morals of those who live with us and present themselves in abundance, as far as is possible. Hence we must keep them before us.[13]

More than a decade after his adoptive father's death, Marcus would still look back upon him as his main role model. We can take him at his word when he says that it is his intention, even as emperor, to "do everything as a disciple of Antoninus."[14] The *Augustan History* confirms that from the time he became Caesar he was determined to "act, speak, and think according to his [adoptive] father's principles."[15]

After praising Antoninus at length, Marcus ends book 1 of the *Meditations* with a note of thanks that he had good servants, friends, and relatives, including good grandfathers.[16] He qualifies this remark, though, with the comment that *nearly* all of them were good. Who then was not deemed good by Marcus? The name most conspicuously absent from the list of individuals Marcus admired in book 1 is that of Hadrian, his adoptive grandfather. Although he mentions Hadrian five times in later chapters, Marcus does so only fleetingly, as an example of a man leveled by death despite his former power and glory.

This omission is even more striking considering the attention lavished on Antoninus's virtues, and it speaks volumes about Marcus's troubled relationship with Emperor Hadrian. Indeed, this is one reason why the *Meditations* is unlikely to have been intended for publication during Marcus's lifetime. The praise heaped on Antoninus inevitably comes across as implying a number of unflattering *contrasts* with his predecessor.[17] In Marcus's telling, Antoninus was everything that Hadrian was not. Hadrian's exclusion would have been perceived as a major slight, a damnatio memoriae. It creates the impression that Marcus had literally nothing good to say about his adoptive grandfather.

Marcus had been reluctant to join the imperial family after watching Hadrian's decline. He was afraid that the office of emperor would corrupt him as well. He would have preferred to live in peace as a philosopher, writing books and frequenting his mother's intellectual salons. Perhaps he would have done so had Antoninus not proved to him that it was possible to live wisely even in a palace. Antoninus was unpretentious, even-tempered, patient, forgiving, and humble; his predecessor was none of these things. Yet the strengths that Antoninus exhibited seemed innate to his character. Marcus was worried that he would not be able to live up to the example set by his adoptive father. He had doubts about his own vanity and temper, among other failings.

Marcus's anxieties about being emperor never entirely went away. Decades later, he was still warning himself to take care not to be "made into a Caesar" by allowing his soul to be dyed with the Tyrian purple of his imperial robes rather than with wisdom. "Strive to continue to be," he admonished himself, "as philosophy wished to make you."[18] Some of Antoninus's imperial predecessors wore ornately embroidered purple robes as a symbol of status. In the eyes of the public this came uneasily close to the regal apparel of a king rather than a first citizen, which is what the emperor was meant to be. Antoninus's preference for plain attire was a signal that he intended to rule as a public servant, in cooperation with the Senate, not as an autocrat modeling himself on absolute monarchs of the kind found among the "barbarians" of eastern kingdoms, such as Parthia.

Marcus lists the qualities he feared he might lose if he allowed royal purple to penetrate his soul. Among them were the natural affection (philostorgia) and kindness that he learned from Lucilla and his Stoic tutors. Whereas his adoptive father ruled with wisdom and justice, Hadrian had been a weak man, intoxicated by his own status, whose frayed mind was eventually dyed purple. Marcus had no intention of turning into another Hadrian. Ironically, he felt that to avoid becoming a Caesar he must "do everything as a disciple of [Emperor] Antoninus."

Marcus's education at this time naturally focused on oratory and speechwriting, arts essential to public office, especially for a future emperor. Indeed, he trained extensively in both Greek and Latin rhetoric. The most acclaimed orators were the Greek Sophists, whose flamboyant and exhilarating lectures covered a range of philosophical teachings, especially concerning virtue. Latin rhetoricians, by contrast, had traditionally focused more on the workmanlike practicalities of Roman legal and political speechwriting. During the Second Sophistic, however, they became more like the crowd-pleasing Greek Sophists; Fronto, like his predecessor Seneca, might plausibly be called a sort of *Latin* Sophist.

Fronto's earliest surviving letter to Marcus has been dated to 139 CE, which suggests he was appointed the young Caesar's tutor not long after Antoninus's accession. Marcus's Greek rhetoric masters are named as Aninius Macer, Caninius Celer, and Herodes Atticus.[19] Although Herodes was the most important of the three, it seems that Antoninus did not recall him from Athens until 140, when the young Caesar was around nineteen.[20] A few years later, in 143, Herodes became consul for the second time, the first Greek ever to be appointed *consul ordinarius*. Fronto, who probably joined the imperial household in 139, is the only Latin rhetorician mentioned as tutor to Marcus. Like Seneca before him, Fronto was a lawyer by profession, rather than a lecturer on rhetoric. He was nevertheless lauded as the finest Latin orator of his day, and even compared to Cicero.[21]

If Marcus had three Greek tutors and only one Latin one, this might have been another consequence of his mother's philhellenism. However, although Fronto is praised briefly in the *Meditations,* no mention is made of Herodes or the other Greek rhetoric tutors.[22] Indeed, Marcus was later thankful to have escaped falling under the spell of Herodes and becoming one of his Sophist disciples.[23] Marcus did not view Latin rhetoric with as much suspicion as he did Greek Sophistry. He heaped more honors on Fronto than on his other rhetoric masters, and he later asked the Senate to erect a statue honoring the rhetorician (probably following his death). We can see from their letters that although Fronto's teaching focused on rhetorical exercises, he did touch on philosophy occasionally. This was almost unavoidable, as some of the Latin texts they studied for their language, such as those of Lucretius, Cicero, and Seneca, mainly concerned philosophical doctrines.

Nevertheless, despite the efforts of these Latin authors, philosophy was still essentially a Greek-language discipline. (That is why Marcus wrote the *Meditations* in Greek.) Having earlier been introduced to a few philosophers by his painting master, Diognetus, Marcus now underwent a more formal program of tuition in the subject. The *Augustan History* names his main philosophy tutors as the Stoics Apollonius of Chalcedon, Sextus of Chaeronea, Junius Rusticus, Claudius Maximus, Cinna Catulus, and the Aristotelian Claudius Severus.[24] Unlike the rhetoricians, each of these men is commemorated in the *Meditations*.

Nearly two centuries earlier, Augustus, the founder of the empire, set a precedent by studying under two Stoic tutors and in his later years encouraging others to read philosophy. Some of his successors followed suit. Emperor Nero, for instance, had the Stoic philosopher Seneca as his rhetoric tutor, although he eventually executed him. Marcus Aurelius, however, had a much more formal and extensive training in Stoicism than any other Roman emperor. Of the five teachers listed, Rusticus and Apollonius were said to have given Marcus the most tuition in philosophy.[25] Marcus wrote that another Stoic, Claudius Maximus, also influenced him very deeply.[26] These three men showed him how to "live in agreement with Nature." They exemplified Stoic philosophy as a way of life, that is, and were guided consistently by reason, rather than by passions such as fear or anger.

Rusticus, Maximus, and Severus were also highly accomplished statesmen, all of whom attained consular rank. We know nothing of Cinna Catulus, although Marcus mentions that Catulus showed him that it was important "to speak well of" one's teachers "as it is reported of Domitius and Athenodotus."[27] Athenodotus was a Stoic teacher from roughly a generation earlier.[28] We do not know who Domitius was, but his name suggests he was a member of the *gens Domitia* and thus a relative of Domitia Lucilla, perhaps an uncle or a cousin. If Lucilla had a devoted student of Stoicism in her extended family, that might help to explain why she involved so many Stoic teachers in her son's education.

Apollonius and Sextus, by contrast, were not statesmen, but professional philosophy lecturers from Greece. (Although he praises Sextus, Marcus may have become his student somewhat later in life.)[29] As a boy, Marcus would have attended Apollonius's lectures on an ad hoc basis. Apollonius returned to Athens toward the end of Hadrian's rule, but Antoninus later recalled him to Rome to supervise Marcus in a more advanced program of philosophical studies.

Apollonius was one of those men who exemplified for Marcus a life dedicated to reason and virtue.[30] As a teacher, he never became irritated with his students. A naturally humble man, Apollonius considered the philosophical expertise and teaching skills, which dazzled his young pupils, the least of his achievements. Nevertheless, this man, fresh from lecturing in Athens, was one of the empire's leading scholars. His emphasis on rational living was typically Stoic. Marcus witnessed him endure severe pain, a lengthy illness, and the loss of a child with unwavering philosophical steadfastness.

Apollonius was the most illustrious of Marcus's philosophy teachers, and the one most responsible for his formal education in Stoicism. Yet not even the influence of this esteemed scholar could explain the transformation Marcus underwent. Something was still missing. Marcus, in fact, received more instruction in Stoicism from Junius Rusticus, "whom he ever revered and whose disciple he became."[31] The exceptional praise heaped on Rusticus in the *Meditations* confirms that he was second only to Antoninus in Marcus's eyes. This raises an intriguing question. Why was the education Marcus Aurelius received from Junius Rusticus so much more important to him than anything he learned from Apollonius and the *other* Stoics?

CHAPTER SEVEN

Disciple of Rusticus

O nce his formal studies in philosophy were under way, Marcus Aurelius began hearing more about a great Stoic philosopher who had recently died at Nicopolis in Greece toward the end of Hadrian's rule. Banished by the emperor Domitian during a political purge four decades earlier, this former slave attracted many students, although he never committed anything to writing. In the years following his demise, his profound wisdom and uniquely powerful voice seemed to have been lost forever.

If the sage of Nicopolis had lived a little longer, Antoninus might have brought him back to Rome along with his fellow Stoic Apollonius. Marcus could, alternatively, have made the pilgrimage east, to sit at the master's feet in Greece. Epictetus, though a near contemporary of Marcus, would later be ranked by him as one of the greatest philosophers in history, alongside Socrates and Chrysippus, the finest scholar of early Stoicism.[1] This demonstrates the exceptionally high regard in which Marcus held Epictetus. (It is as striking as comparing a modern-day playwright to Shakespeare.)

The young Caesar felt himself to have narrowly missed out on the opportunity to meet the most revered philosopher of his age.

Junius Rusticus would surely have quoted Epictetus to Marcus, which doubtless infuriated him, as Rusticus's remarks were often intended to challenge Marcus's conceit. Rusticus would proclaim, in his typically outspoken way, that it was nothing but foolish vanity for his student to wear his imperial purple robes around the palace. Even the emperor, Antoninus, dressed for the most part like an ordinary senator. We don't know what their tense exchanges about Marcus's youthful vanity were like. "But I am Caesar!" we might imagine him snapping. "On the contrary," Rusticus may have replied, smiling, "you are a weak little soul, carrying around a corpse, who believes himself to be Caesar."[2] If these are the sort of teachings Rusticus derived from Epictetus, it is easy to see why a Roman noble of Marcus's status would have found them so challenging. Nevertheless, they remained close. Rusticus provoked Marcus's temper, but he also showed him how to restore friendship after a quarrel.

During Hadrian's early stays in Greece, perhaps when he served as archon of Athens, around 112, he attended Epictetus's lectures.[3] Hadrian reputedly became friends — hard though this is to imagine — with Epictetus, and at some point also met one of his most devoted students, a Greek writer named Arrian, to whom we owe our knowledge of Epictetus's thought. After he was acclaimed emperor, Hadrian promoted Arrian, making him suffect consul in 130. (Two ordinary consuls, *consules ordinarii*, were elected each January and normally served for one year, but if one resigned or passed away the senator who filled his role for the remainder of his term assumed the slightly less prestigious title *suffect consul*.) Eventually Arrian was appointed prefect of Cappadocia, one of the most senior posts in the Roman military. The first we hear of Marcus's philosophy teacher Junius Rusticus is *his* appointment as suffect consul under Hadrian soon after this, in 133.

The missing link between Epictetus and Marcus Aurelius comes from a remarkable statement about Arrian and Rusticus made by a fourth-century Roman orator called Themistius, who vividly describes how military service brought these two famous Stoics together.

[The emperors Hadrian, Antoninus, and Marcus Aurelius] pulled Arrian and Rusticus away from their books, refusing to let them be mere pen-and-ink philosophers. They did not let them write about courage and stay at home, or compose legal treatises while avoiding the public domain that is law's concern, or decide what form of government is best while abstaining from any participation in government. The emperors to whom I am now alluding consequently escorted these men to the general's tent as well as to the speaker's platform. In their role as Roman generals, these men passed through the Caspian Gates, drove the Alani out of Armenia, and established boundaries for the Iberians and the Albani.[4]

In other words, Rusticus served alongside Arrian, in 135, during Rome's war against the Alani, an aggressive tribe of Sarmatian nomads. The Alani had crossed the Caucasus mountain range to attack the Roman client state of Armenia via neighboring Caucasian Iberia (Eastern Georgia) and Caucasian Albania (Azerbaijan). Arrian was in command of the three Cappadocian legions, whereas Rusticus, being a younger man of consular rank, presumably served under him as a legionary legate. We can only imagine the conversations these two famous Stoics must have had during their military service together. It may even have been Arrian who first introduced Rusticus to Stoic philosophy by handing him a copy of his private notes on Epictetus's lectures.

Marcus Aurelius would later express gratitude for the fact that Rusticus gave him a copy of certain notes (*hypomnemata*), from his private collection, containing the teachings of Epictetus. This was quite possibly one of the most significant events in Marcus's life, at least in relation to his love of philosophy. As he elsewhere quotes repeatedly from the *Discourses* transcribed by Arrian we can assume that this was the book Rusticus gave him. There were originally eight volumes of the *Discourses,* though only four survive today. As well as quoting from the four extant books, Marcus also seems to attribute otherwise unknown sayings and passages to Epictetus. This suggests that he read the four missing volumes of Epictetus's *Discourses.* Yet for a time, perhaps until they reached Marcus and his court, almost no one knew such writings existed. Indeed, when Arrian later published the *Discourses,* he added a preface stressing that they were originally intended to be circulated privately among his closest friends. "I do not know how they fell into the hands of the public," he says, "without either my consent or my knowledge."[5]

Marcus particularly admired Rusticus for his frank and unpretentious manner, typical of a Stoic and quite a contrast with the Sophists. Marcus refers in particular to a letter of unknown date addressed to Lucilla, his mother, which exemplified the sort of straight talking of which we know she approved.[6] Rusticus sent it from the coastal town of Sinuessa, which lies on the Appian Way, the road connecting Rome with the Adriatic port of Brundisium (modern-day Brindisi). He was perhaps writing to Lucilla on his return from the East, shortly after Arrian's victory in the war against the Alani. It was customary for educated Romans to send letters ahead announcing their arrival, and notifying the recipient of their desire to meet in person. Marcus would have been turning fifteen, and already had a passion for philosophy. The simple frankness of this letter must have impressed Lucilla as a relief from the verbal chicanery of the Sophists. Maybe for this reason, fresh from the war, and his conversations with Arrian, Rusticus was appointed by Lucilla to serve as her son's private tutor in Stoicism.

Marcus got two things from Rusticus that he did not get from Apollonius or his other Stoic tutors. The first was the copy of the *Discourses* of Epictetus, which Rusticus presumably brought back from the East, having acquired it in person from his former commander.[7] The *Discourses* contained something rather different from the Stoicism Marcus had thus far been learning. Marcus's main philosophy teacher at this time was Apollonius, whom he mentions in his letters to Fronto.[8] The rhetorician appears to be mocking Apollonius, therefore, when he writes to Marcus:

> To be sure you would read a book to your philosopher; listen in silence while your master explained it; shew by nods that you understood him; while others were reading, you would yourself mostly sleep; would hear reiterated at length and often: "What is the first premise? What is the second?" with windows wide open, hear the point labored, "If it is day, it is light."[9]

Fronto jokes that Marcus would leave such lessons carefree, having nothing to work on and no progress to demonstrate to his teacher. His point was that such philosophical lectures are mostly theory, whereas oratory, as he saw it, is a practical art.

While Marcus does praise Apollonius for embodying Stoicism in his way of life, Fronto's caricature implies that Apollonius did not concern himself much with the behavior of his students outside the classroom. In stark contrast, Arrian portrays his teacher Epictetus challenging his students, often in very emphatic terms, to exercise wisdom and virtue consistently throughout their daily lives.[10] Although his language was not as polished as that of an orator, Epictetus sought, like Socrates before him, to transform the character of his students by directly questioning their deeply held beliefs and values. His words had a profound psychological impact: "If, indeed, these *Discourses* should produce this effect, they will have, I think, the result which the words of philosophers ought to have. But if they shall not, let those who read them know that, when Epictetus delivered them, the hearer could not avoid being affected in the way that Epictetus wished him to be."[11] Marcus, I suspect, was similarly affected, and inspired to work at improving his own character after Rusticus introduced him to the *Discourses*. For Epictetus, training in Stoicism focused squarely on moral self-examination, endurance, self-discipline, and emotional resilience. It was, in other words, not abstract and theoretical but deeply personal and *therapeutic* in orientation.

Epictetus himself had studied Stoic philosophy under the Roman equestrian Musonius Rufus, who used to say something that would never have been heard from a Sophist: "If you have leisure to praise me, I am speaking to no purpose." Epictetus said of his teacher: "Accordingly he used to speak in such a way that every one of us who was sitting there supposed that someone had accused him before Rufus: he so touched on what was doing, he so placed before the eyes every man's faults. The philosopher's school is a doctor's clinic: you ought not to go out of it with pleasure, but with pain."[12] Was this what it was like for Marcus as a Stoic student of Rusticus? The emphasis on pinpointing and radically challenging individual students' character flaws could not be farther removed from the dull public lectures on Stoic logic that Fronto describes Marcus as having attended.

If the first thing Marcus obtained from Rusticus was a copy of Epictetus's *Discourses*, the second was this notion of Stoic philosophy as a form of psychological therapy. The *Meditations* explicitly states that it was Rusticus who first taught Marcus that his character needed improvement and, indeed, "therapy" (*therapeia*).[13] Many people today mistakenly assume that psychotherapy began with Sigmund Freud and his method of psychoanalysis.[14] Yet it had always been common in Greek literature to employ a medical model of philosophy, frequently presenting it as a sort of "medicine" for the soul. Socrates' trademark method of questioning, the elenchus, for instance, was described as a cure for intellectual conceit, resembling a pharmaceutical remedy, though the ingredients were words not drugs – a "talking cure" as we would say today.[15] Of all the ancient schools of philosophy, Stoicism was the one most associated with the notion of philosophy as a therapy for the mind (*psyche*). The Stoics wrote books on philosophical therapy and psychopathology, such as the once famous *Therapeutics* of Chrysippus, which like most of these early works is now lost. Roman authors made use of the same medical analogy. Seneca's *On Anger,* indeed, survives to this day, and lucidly explains how Stoic therapy of the passions was applied in practice.

What then was the main "presenting problem" which troubled Marcus and for which he sought therapy? We can look for hints in the passage that first mentions Stoic therapeia and the areas in which Rusticus instructed him. On close examination, Rusticus appears to have helped Marcus first and foremost to overcome two vices, which are often found together: *vanity* and *anger.* The positive changes Rusticus helped Marcus achieve also resemble the qualities he admired in Antoninus and others. Through Stoic therapy, in other words, he became more like his own role models.

As we have seen, Epictetus warned his students that having their flaws pointed out, though therapeutic, was often painful. At one point, Marcus compares the challenge of gently correcting someone's moral behavior to that of tactfully pointing out another person's bad breath or body odor without irritating him.[16] We can see, then, why Rusticus's therapeutic interventions may have provoked his anger at times but also why Marcus may have been grateful to him. Indeed, it was Rusticus, the man with whom Marcus most often clashed, who showed him how to recover his composure and be reconciled with his friends. According to Epictetus, the ideal Stoic is able to deal calmly and wisely with arguments; he neither fights with anyone nor, if he is able, does he permit others to fight. First and foremost, he says, Socrates, was never irritated in an argument, he never uttered abuse or resorted to insults, but instead he endured the abusive behavior of others and, where possible, brought an end to quarrels.[17] Epictetus therefore suggests that the main thing his students need to learn from Socrates is a particular sort of temperance, the ability to tolerate disagreement without turning it into a fight.

Such also was the main lesson Marcus recalled learning from another of his Stoic tutors, Cinna Catulus.[18] Catulus taught Marcus to pay attention when his friends pointed out his faults because even if their criticisms seemed unjustified, by listening patiently to them he might learn how to restore their friendship. Rusticus must have taught him more or less the same thing. Marcus was able to model similar traits by observing the behavior of his adoptive father. Antoninus was exceptionally tolerant of free speech. He welcomed disagreement, and thanked others for correcting him. He would even listen to those who criticized him unjustly without criticizing them in return.[19] Marcus exhibits many of these qualities in his private correspondence with Fronto, and they would stand him in good stead as a diplomat and negotiator later in life.

Marcus states that Rusticus also had to warn him against behaving like a Sophist. His love of oratory was, at times, motivated by vanity. Rusticus noticed this and accused him of using poetry and rhetoric simply to impress others. The Sophists were apt to give moralizing sermons about virtue, but they often made no effort to live up to their own teachings. Rusticus convinced Marcus that this was a waste of his talents; rather than posing as a good man he should focus on *becoming* one — on transforming his character through training in philosophy.

Marcus's letters to Fronto at this time are full of vivid pictures revealing the minutiae of the young Caesar's family life, as well as hints of his philosophical progress. In one rather slapstick vignette, Marcus describes the chaos brought about by his sister Annia's severe menstrual pains:

> This is how I have passed the last few days. My sister was seized suddenly with such pain in the privy parts that it was dreadful to see her. Morcover, my mother, in the flurry of the moment, inadvertently ran her side against a corner of the wall, causing us as well as herself great pain by the accident. For myself, when I went to lie down I came upon a scorpion in my bed; however, I was in time to kill it before lying down upon it.[20]

In his reply, Fronto avers that Marcus's Stoic training would have prepared him to remain calm: "I am truly thankful to the Gods that they have kept you safe and unharmed. You, I make no doubt, were unperturbed, for I know your philosophic views; for myself, however much you wiseacres may laugh at me, I confess I was thoroughly shocked."[21] By now, Marcus's friends evidently perceived him to be a devoted student of Stoicism who was already on the way to mastering the Stoics' characteristic apatheia, freedom from emotional distress. Yet it is clear from Marcus's correspondence with Fronto that the young Caesar increasingly felt torn between his initial attraction to rhetoric and his growing commitment to the ideals of Stoic philosophy. A sort of contest developed between Fronto, his favorite rhetoric teacher, and Rusticus, his Stoic mentor, as though they were fighting over their student's very soul. Eventually, Marcus could not bear it any longer, and the conflict led to a dramatic emotional crisis.

Until this escalated, everything had been going well. At the start of 145, Marcus was appointed consul for a second time, alongside Antoninus, who now served his third consulship. In April, Marcus and Faustina were finally wed, as she had reached the age of fourteen. Yet something changed shortly after the wedding that left Marcus deeply unsettled. He had been reading the works of an author named Aristo, an early Greek Stoic who broke away from Zeno to embrace a simpler and more austere philosophy, not unlike Cynicism.[22] Marcus, now twenty-five, wrote to Fronto in anguish.[23]

He began by assuring Fronto that Aristo's books were helping him become a better person and find a better way of life. At the same time, though, he felt ashamed of himself and grew frustrated because his character fell short of his ideals. Marcus described being distraught, vacillating between anger and sadness, and he had even lost his appetite. He apologizes for not writing to Fronto sooner because he was so preoccupied by this inner turmoil. In particular, he had become convinced that it was wrong to defend both sides of an argument, an exercise commonly practiced by ancient rhetoricians and lawyers.

It is my impression that Marcus initially saw Fronto as someone who was unlike the Greek Sophists. Fronto kept insisting that he was helping Marcus use eloquent language not just to win acclaim but in order to express philosophical truths more clearly. Yet over time, Marcus came to realize that Fronto was more concerned with persuasion than with the love of truth. Fronto, like the Greek Sophists, would say whatever he felt an audience wanted to hear —

praising Hadrian in the Senate, for instance, but criticizing him after he was dead. Speaking out of both sides of one's mouth was something no Stoic could abide.

Although we are told that Marcus had been fascinated by philosophy since he was twelve, this moment more than a decade later is often taken to be the point at which he finally embraced Stoicism wholeheartedly. Perhaps after introducing Marcus to the *Discourses* of Epictetus, Rusticus lent him the writings of Aristo. Fronto later mentions that Marcus has abandoned his formal training in rhetoric, and their correspondence seems to have become less frequent. Fronto insists that Rusticus was forced, nevertheless, to concede "with a frown" that Marcus still retained a natural flair for giving speeches. The rhetorician acknowledged with sadness, that "that friend of mine, the Roman Rusticus," who would "gladly surrender and sacrifice his life for your little finger," had finally won Marcus over completely to Stoic philosophy as a way of life.[24]

CHAPTER EIGHT

The Two Emperors

"Do not expect the ideal Republic of the philosophers to happen overnight," Marcus told himself, "but be content if even small steps go well, and consider that to be no small matter."[1] Gnaeus Claudius Severus Arabianus was a Roman statesman and another of Marcus Aurelius's philosophy tutors. The two men called each other "brother," and Severus's son would eventually marry one of Marcus's daughters. Severus, an Aristotelian, tutored Marcus in political philosophy. He taught him about several philosophers associated with Roman republican values and opposition to political tyranny, including the Stoic Cato the Younger, who opposed Julius Caesar; Brutus, one of Caesar's lead assassins; and Thrasea, a Stoic senator was executed for his opposition to Emperor Nero.

Marcus had found it difficult to understand how the office of emperor could be prevented from degenerating into a form of political tyranny. Severus persuaded him that an empire could exist "which respects most of all the freedom of the governed." Together they envisioned a utopian political state ruled by a mixed government, "in which there is the same law for all, one administered with regard to equal rights and equal freedom of speech."[2]

It is difficult to know how Marcus imagined this philosophical ideal, which seems radically egalitarian, being applied in practice to the political realities of the principate. He did watch his adoptive father, Antoninus, take important steps, though, toward *sharing* power rather than ruling as an autocrat. Whereas Hadrian had become increasingly authoritarian and alienated from the people, Antoninus saw himself more as their servant. As emperor, it was said, he treated the Senate with the same respect that he had desired from the emperor when he was a senator himself.[3] Antoninus consulted frequently with senators, obtaining their approval before making important decisions, and Marcus would later follow his example. Marcus, and perhaps Antoninus before him, even viewed the public treasury as belonging to the Senate and would request permission to use its funds.[4]

Marcus's transition from the role of Caesar to that of emperor happened more gradually than is generally assumed. It began when he and Faustina had their first child. Two years into their marriage, in late 147, a daughter was born. Antoninus immediately granted Marcus, as Caesar, the tribunician power and the proconsular power outside the city, with the additional right of making five proposals in the Senate. (The Senate as a whole deliberated upon legislation, which could be proposed only by certain of its members including senior magistrates, such as the praetors and consuls.) Around the same time, Faustina was designated an Augusta. This title, akin to "empress," could also be held by the emperor's daughter or by the wife of a deceased emperor. Although still only a Caesar, Marcus now wielded the key imperial powers and was at least nominally married to an empress.

These new powers and titles meant that for the last thirteen years of his adoptive father's rule, Marcus was not only Antoninus's righthand man, he was also his co-emperor in all but name. From that time, the emperor made no promotions without consulting his adoptive son. Marcus was highly committed to his duties and an active deputy ruler. The policies of Rome during this period may therefore tentatively be viewed as evidence of the political values that Antoninus shared with Marcus.

These were perhaps Marcus's happiest years, his time divided between imperial duties and family life at Rome. Between 149 and 152, Faustina gave birth to twin sons, followed by two more daughters, and then another son.[5] Around 155, though, Marcus's mother died. She had been living with his adoptive family in the House of Tiberius, and Marcus later gave thanks that "though it was my mother's fate to die young, she spent the last years of her life with me."[6] Shortly after Domitia Lucilla's death, Marcus also lost his only sibling, his younger sister. Suddenly every link to his birth family, with whom he had sought refuge from the stress of court life, was gone forever.

In 159 and 160, Faustina had two more daughters. She would give birth to at least fourteen children over the course of her marriage, including two sets of twins. Around half of these children died while Faustina and Marcus were still alive. Coins issued during the period commemorate the *fecunditas Augustae,* the fertility of the empress, a quality greatly esteemed by the Roman people – although it is hard to imagine what life must have been like for Faustina. She would have been pregnant almost half of her marriage from the birth of their first child until that of their last, twenty-three years later. In the *Meditations,* apart from a possible reference to her being with child again, Marcus says nothing about his wife except to thank the gods that she was "so loyal, so naturally affectionate [philostorgos], so genuine."[7] He seems sincere in his praise of Faustina, privately attributing qualities to her similar to those possessed by his mother and lacking, according to Fronto, in most other Roman nobles.

Antoninus had been appointed emperor in part because Marcus was still a youth, and a suitable interim ruler was required. Hadrian, who died at sixty-two, had no reason to anticipate that his successor would reach the venerable age of seventy-four; Antoninus ended up ruling for twenty-three years. Although he took good care of his health, he suffered recurring headaches and chronic back problems toward the end of his life. He became so bent over that splints had to be bound to his torso to enable him to walk upright. Nevertheless, he seldom called on physicians and continued to work tirelessly. He could rely wholeheartedly on Marcus, who served an apprenticeship of unprecedented length by his side.

Emperor Antoninus Pius died in March 161 at his ancestral villa in Lorium, after a bout of fever and vomiting caused by some Alpine cheese he had eaten. Such a demise would normally provoke accusations of deliberate poisoning, but none of the sources mention rumors to that effect. We are told instead that Antoninus's last act was to order his Praetorian prefects to acclaim Marcus as emperor. He marked the handover by having a golden statue of the goddess Fortuna, which belonged in the emperor's chambers, moved to Marcus's room. For a spell, Antoninus's mind had become troubled by the fever, but he regained his composure. He gave the nightwatch officer the password *aequanimitas,* then turned over and drifted into a sleep from which he never awoke.

"Equanimity" perfectly summed up the public's perception of Antoninus's character and rule. From his adoptive father, Marcus learned that with patience and an even temper the Roman Empire could be governed wisely, and its people ruled justly. In stark contrast to his predecessor, Antoninus was deified by the Senate without hesitation: "All men vied with one another to give him honor, and all extolled his devoutness, his mercy, his intelligence, and his righteousness."[8] Antoninus had ruled the empire for longer than any man since its founder, Augustus. Yet no voices clamored for change, although such cries had usually grown louder toward the end of previous regimes. His time in power was not without its challenges, of course, including floods, famines, buildings being ravaged by fire and collapsing, and earthquakes that destroyed whole towns.

This was the pinnacle of the Pax Romana, an era during which the empire flourished and enjoyed prolonged peace. Hadrian, to his credit, had left behind a tightly organized state with efficient military defenses. Antoninus, known for his diplomatic expertise, dealt wisely with unrest within the empire. "Rebellions, wherever they occurred," it was said, "he suppressed not by means of cruelty, but with moderation and dignity."[9] He did wage some wars remotely through his legates, such as the one which extended Roman control beyond Hadrian's Wall into lowland Scotland and led to the construction of the Antonine Wall.[10] Yet he generally maintained peace on the empire's frontiers and in neighboring states without resorting to arms. Indeed, Antoninus loved to quote an old slogan: *he would rather save a single citizen than slay a thousand foes.*[11] "No one has ever had such prestige among foreign nations as he," enthuses the *Augustan History*. Marcus Aurelius inherited the empire in this enviable condition.[12]

After the death of Antoninus, Marcus at first wanted to retreat from public life and "abandon himself to philosophy," perhaps hoping that Lucius Verus, who was next in line, might assume the throne instead. The Senate, however, pleaded with him to become emperor.[13] He agreed on condition that they confer similar powers upon his adoptive brother. Marcus took the cognomen "Antoninus" to signify continuity between his rule and that of his adoptive father but chose to drop "Aelius," the family name of Hadrian. The titles Imperator and Augustus, and the tribunician power, were shared with his brother.

This was the first time that two Roman emperors had ruled side by side, although power had been shared before, as when Marcus wielded key imperial powers as Caesar under Antoninus. When the early Romans deposed their last king, Tarquin the Proud, according to legend they replaced him with two consuls. To keep either from abusing his power, the two men together presided over the Senate, and each could veto the other's motions. The consulship had been shared from that time forward. So, although novel, the idea of joint rule by two emperors was not unprecedented. It may be that by sharing the tribunician power Marcus and Lucius were likewise able, theoretically, to check each other's control of the Senate. This may have been viewed as a safeguard against the office of emperor degenerating into a form of one-man rule. Senators would have recalled how Antoninus, wielding imperial powers as Caesar, was able to save many of their lives by staying Hadrian's hand during the final weeks of his life.

Marcus, nevertheless, commanded more authority (*auctoritas*) than Lucius. He was always named first on inscriptions. In the year of Antoninus's death, the two both served as consuls, Lucius for a second time and Marcus for a third, which gave him seniority in the Senate. Marcus was also pontifex maximus, the supreme priest of the Roman religion, a post only ever held by one man at a time. Whereas Marcus had long been wedded to Faustina, Antoninus's daughter and an Augusta, Lucius was a bachelor until his accession at age thirty. At that time he was betrothed to Marcus's eleven-year-old daughter, Lucilla, though he would have to wait three years to marry her.[14] Marcus, although he now dropped his family name,

Verus, bestowed it on Lucius, as if he had become his adopted *son* rather than his brother.[15] Despite being nominally a second Augustus, therefore, Lucius was effectively Marcus's deputy, wielding power under him somewhat like a proconsul, or provincial governor.[16]

Marcus was nearly a decade older than Lucius and suffered from notoriously poor health, while Lucius was known for his vigor and love of sports. Lucius was therefore expected to outlive his brother and, in that sense, presumably succeed him as sole emperor, or senior co-emperor ruling alongside one of Marcus's sons. Lucius was also popular, for he had more of the common touch than Marcus. Although Antoninus had been closer to Marcus, he was fond of Lucius's frank and down-to-earth attitude, which he had encouraged Marcus to emulate.[17] Lucius, though, never warmed to Antoninus, showing him loyalty rather than genuine affection.[18]

In adulthood, especially as emperor, Lucius began to enjoy a kind of celebrity status. He was a tall man, with a good physique. His prominent brow gave him a stately appearance. He was so proud of his blond hair that he allegedly sprinkled it with gold dust to add to its luster.[19] From the surviving sculptures we can see that Lucius styled his facial hair in a manner not unlike that of his natural father, Lucius Aelius Caesar. However, he grew it much longer, in a rakish style that recalled the unkempt look of some "barbarian" races.[20]

Lucius was only eight years old when he was adopted into the imperial family. Whenever they traveled, Marcus shared Antoninus's carriage. Lucius always journeyed with one of the Praetorian prefects, an arrangement that for more than two decades provided him with a unique opportunity to bond with Rome's senior army officers. Lucius's natural father had commanded a legion in Pannonia for about a year, gaining credit for a few modest victories. Soldiers often held high hopes for the young sons of their favorite generals, and the Praetorians must have warmed to young Lucius as he grew up under the wing of their commander, perhaps even adopting the boy as their mascot. As an adult, moreover, Lucius was considered "better suited for military enterprises" than Marcus, due to his relative youth and good health.[21] Despite lacking military experience, he would serve as his brother's representative with the legions.

After they were proclaimed co-emperors by the Senate, Lucius rode with Marcus to deliver their accession speech to the soldiers assembled on the parade ground of the *castra praetoria* outside Rome.[22] Marcus asked Lucius to address them on his behalf and offer each a donative of five thousand denarii, approximately five years' pay, plus extra for the officers. It had become a necessary evil for new emperors to buy the Praetorians' loyalty since the accession of Claudius, who gave them less than four thousand denarii each. On this occasion, the Praetorians may simply have expected more money from two emperors than from one. The soldiers roared their approval, acclaiming the brothers Imperatores. Marcus already anticipated, though, that the loyalty of his Praetorian cohorts might soon be tested on a campaign in the distant East.

CHAPTER NINE

The Parthian Invasion

In the hours preceding his death, Emperor Antoninus, delirious with fever, temporarily lost his characteristic equanimity. He became agitated, and his ravings seemed to take on a prophetic quality as he spoke out angrily against certain kings.[1] Vologases IV of the Arsacid dynasty, king of Parthia, was undoubtedly one of the names on the dying emperor's lips.

Antoninus had taught Marcus "to anticipate events in the distant future" and assume a long-term perspective on the governance of the empire.[2] Stoics such as Junius Rusticus had taught him to adopt a philosophical attitude toward events beyond his direct control, "neither crushed by the present nor fearing the future."[3] As the emperor lay dying, his adoptive son and deputy had been long prepared to assume power. Both men sensed, though, that the era of peace, lasting two decades, with which Antoninus's rule had become synonymous was about to be shattered.

Antoninus himself had never fought a war, though his legates had put down uprisings in the eastern empire among the Jews, as well as in Achaea (Greece) and Egypt. He preferred to secure peace by means of diplomacy. Around 139 he had persuaded King Ma'nu VIII, for instance, who ruled the kingdom of Osroene, to switch his allegiance from Parthia to Rome.[4] Osroene was an important buffer state, strategically located between Syria and Armenia. A coin dated to around 141–143 also shows Antoninus crowning a new client king of Armenia, a Roman consul called Sohaemus.

Although Antoninus established treaties with several eastern rulers, he pointedly refused to return the golden throne of Parthia, despite the pleas of its envoys.[5] This treasured artifact had been captured several decades earlier by Trajan and shipped from Ctesiphon to Rome, where it was exhibited as a war trophy. Returning it would have strengthened the authority of King Vologases over rival Parthian dynasties, and Antoninus knew all too well that a united Parthia would present a major threat on Rome's eastern frontier.

The Parthians were originally a nomadic warrior race of steppe horsemen. The region they controlled had formerly been the Persian Empire, conquered by Alexander the Great in the fourth century BCE. Over the intervening centuries, the kingdoms founded by Alexander's successors slowly collapsed, and the Parthians found themselves in control of many wealthy Hellenistic cities, along the lucrative silk routes between Rome and the far eastern kingdoms of India and China. Although the Parthians had never succeeded in capturing much territory from the Romans, they were considered Rome's closest military rival, having dealt them several humiliating defeats in the past.

In 151 CE, Vologases captured the independent Parthian kingdom of Characene, in Lower Mesopotamia, from a rival Arsacid king. Its capital was a prosperous seaport located near the mouths the Euphrates and Tigris, from which cargo ships sailed through the Persian Gulf heading for India. Flushed with victory, Vologases then threatened to invade Armenia, the most important Roman client state in the East. Antoninus sent him a letter that somehow dissuaded him.[6] The emperor knew, though, that a Parthian invasion had only been forestalled. As the *Augustan History* put it, Vologases planned the Parthian War under Antoninus Pius that he would declare under Lucius Verus and Marcus Aurelius.[7]

Marcus was already facing problems. As soon as he took the throne, it seemed, the gods began putting his Stoicism to the test.[8] First came the most severe flooding of the Tiber in living memory. For days until the waters receded, the city was awash with filth, debris, raw sewage, and the bloated corpses of drowned animals. Many buildings were destroyed, the majority of them Rome's notoriously unstable *insulae,* apartment blocks housing common people. The city was in chaos, and the cleanup would have lasted months, while houses crumbled, produce spoiled, and livestock lay dying. As if this were not enough, the flood brought disease and a major famine in its wake.

Rome had the resources to endure such catastrophes. Marcus did his best to aid the city's recovery by ordering grain from the warehouses distributed to the starving populace. The real threat, however, was political. Whenever "Father Tiber" flooded, ordinary Romans saw it as a punishment from the gods, an omen that fostered concerns about the incumbent emperor, who was also their high priest. Marcus was fortunate that on August 31, 161, in the wake of this disaster, Faustina gave birth to twin boys. This was cause for public celebration, as it provided a sign that the emperor was still blessed by the gods.

The empress had previously lost several children. During this pregnancy she dreamt that she was giving birth to two serpents, one stronger and more ferocious than the other. One of the twin boys she bore, indeed, died four years later. The surviving brother had been given the same name that his uncle Lucius Verus received decades earlier when he was adopted into the imperial family: Lucius Aelius Aurelius Commodus. We know him simply as Commodus.

While the city was still celebrating the birth of the twin boys in the autumn of 161, word arrived that Vologases had invaded Armenia. This was alarming news. Rome had first learned to fear the Parthians in the era of the late republic when they defeated the entire army of Marcus Licinius Crassus, at the Battle of Carrhae in 53 BCE.[9] Crassus, the newly appointed governor of Syria, had marched seven legions across the Euphrates into Upper Mesopotamia, where he was tricked into engaging with a small Parthian force near Edessa, the capital of Osroene. The Parthians were natural horsemen, and their agile mounts, familiarity with the terrain, and ability to find water, gave them a major logistical advantage. The Roman legions were forced to camp near cities and march along the banks of rivers to keep themselves hydrated. Crassus made the fatal mistake of sending his infantry, parched from the sun and exhausted by marching, into battle out on the Parthian steppe. Crassus was killed along with twenty thousand of his soldiers, and a further ten thousand were enslaved. This, Rome's first major defeat by Parthia, had never been forgotten. It must have weighed on Marcus's mind as he pondered his response to Vologases' invasion.

The challenge of beating the Parthian cavalry in a pitched battle remained virtually unaltered two hundred years later. The Parthians possessed stronger, higher-carbon steel than the Romans. Parthian scale armor was hard to penetrate, and their arrowheads could pierce through the legionary *scutum*, a lightweight wooden shield. The majority of Parthian troops were lightly armored mounted archers, armed with powerful recurve bows. They were supported by heavy cavalry, or "cataphracts," the forerunners of medieval European knights. These riders wielded heavy, two-handed lances, reputedly capable of impaling two men at once. Fronto compared Parthian cataphracts – on warhorses covered in scale barding (body armor), charging into battle against the Roman infantry – to gigantic finned monsters plunging beneath the ocean waves.[10]

The Parthians' favorite tactic was to surround their enemy quickly on horseback, bombarding them with a hail of arrows. If their opponents tried to stand their ground and wait out the onslaught, the Parthians would be resupplied from camels bearing seemingly endless quantities of ammunition. If the enemy charged, the Parthian archers would make a tactical withdrawal, quickly riding away to a safe distance. They had perfected a technique known as the "Parthian shot" (from which the term "parting shot" derives). By using their stirrups to remain stable, riders would turn around in the saddle, face backward, and fire on their enemy while riding away. If the enemy infantry did manage to close with them, the Parthian bowmen would be shielded by heavy cataphract lancers, charging to devastating effect, breaking up the infantry formations and leaving them vulnerable to another hail of arrows.

By the time news of the Parthian attack arrived at Rome, two weeks later, Vologases had already taken Artaxata, the capital of Armenia. He deposed the client king appointed decades earlier by Antoninus and replaced him with another member of Parthia's Arsacid dynasty. Marcus would have to wait until the following March for the spring campaign season to begin. The delay, however, allowed him time to prepare his eastern armies and plan a counteroffensive, but before he had a chance to issue any orders, a bizarre catastrophe altered the course of the war.

The mystic Alexander of Abonoteichus was one of the most colorful characters of the Antonine age. The best description of him comes from *Alexander the False Prophet*, a satire by the second-century rhetorician Lucian. Alexander became rich and famous by founding an oracular cult around 150–160 CE based on the worship of a snake god with long hair and human ears. Glycon, or "Sweetie," as he was called, was supposedly the offspring of Aesculapius, the god of medicine, which would make him a grandson of the Olympian deity Apollo.

Although Lucian's story might strike us as somewhat fanciful, the cult's popularity has been confirmed by archaeological and numismatic evidence. Lucian claimed that Glycon was an elaborate hand puppet, and denounced the oracle as a total sham. He wrote that Alexander used to wrap a real python around himself while concealing its head, so he could display instead a puppet head. When questions were presented by gullible supplicants in a dimly lit room full of incense smoke, an assistant concealed behind a curtain would pronounce Glycon's answers through a hidden tube attached to the puppet's mouth.[11]

Alexander's cult had spread rapidly beyond his home province of Bithynia and Pontus, especially after his daughter married his most influential devotee, the governor of the Roman province of Asia. The governor of another nearby province, Marcus Sedatus Severianus, proconsul of Cappadocia, decided to consult Glycon about the Parthian invasion. The oracle proclaimed that if Severianus attacked without delay, Armenia and Parthia would be cowed by Rome's "mighty spear." Severianus, with spectacular credulity, launched an impulsive campaign against the Parthians, unauthorized by Marcus.

This reckless folly led to one of the worst military defeats since Carrhae—Lucian called it simply "the Armenian disaster."[12] Severianus marched a legion from Cappadocia into western Armenia attempting to reclaim the strategically important city of Elegia. Once there, though, his men were encircled by the forces of a senior

Parthian general called Chosroes. After three days of fighting, Servianus was defeated and fell upon his sword in dishonor.[13] His troops were massacred under a hail of Parthian arrows.[14] The humiliating loss of an entire legion devastated Roman morale, and delayed Marcus and Lucius's counteroffensive, perhaps even prolonging the war by several years.

Emboldened by this fortuitous victory, the Parthians crossed the Euphrates and invaded the Roman province of Syria. The garrison there had not fought a major battle against Parthia since Trajan's campaign nearly half a century earlier. Its men were completely undisciplined and out of shape. Legions stationed on the European mainland were often on maneuvers, carrying out drills in the countryside. Scarcity of drinking water in the East meant that Roman soldiers were allowed to pass their time in the cities, frequenting taverns and brothels.

The governor of Syria, Lucius Attidius Cornelianus, whose soldiers were among those serving their time by idling in towns, was next to suffer a major defeat. One of his legions was routed and forced to retreat, possibly to the fortress of Samosata. The Parthians then wrested control from the Romans of several fortified cities along the Euphrates. At the same time, worries arose about a popular uprising against Roman rule in Syria. It can be assumed that some civilians took sides with the Parthians; soldiers might also have mutinied or been on the verge of doing so. Rome was suddenly in danger of losing the whole region to Vologases.

The co-emperors began planning a new counteroffensive. Severianus had rushed into his disastrous attack against the Parthians with a single legion. Marcus's extensive preparations for the next phase in the Parthian War clearly demonstrate how dramatically his proconsul had underestimated Rome's adversary. First and foremost, Marcus and Lucius decided that one of them must journey east. Many common soldiers believed, or at least hoped, that an army led by an emperor was invincible, since the gods would be on his side.[15] (Most emperors, of course, were unlikely to station themselves near the front unless confident of victory.) The army's morale could therefore be improved simply by the sight of their ruler and his Praetorian cohorts.[16]

Lucius was placed in command of the Parthian War, and departed for Antioch, in Syria, to set up headquarters. Marcus later hinted that he oversaw the war remotely from Rome, which may be partly true.[17] Even using the empire's highly efficient horse-relay communications system, though, it would take about thirteen days, each way, to send messages back and forth to Antioch. Supreme command in the East must therefore have been delegated to Lucius, although he, in turn, left many decisions to his generals. Nevertheless, this would become known as the Parthian War of Lucius Verus, and to a large extent it defined his term as co-emperor.[18]

Lucius was accompanied by the Praetorian prefect Furius Victorinus, a contingent of guards, and a retinue of courtiers, the companions of the emperor (*comites*). Victorinus and Lucius, as noted, were probably close friends, for they had been traveling companions for years before Lucius became emperor. Marcus also sent his paternal cousin, the consul Marcus Annius Libo, to keep an eye on Lucius. Although Libo lacked military experience, Marcus appointed him to replace the military governor of Syria. He also replaced the fallen proconsul Severianus with the veteran commander Marcus Statius Priscus, the governor of Britain. This move gives a flavor of the logistical challenges Marcus faced: it would have taken Priscus nearly two months to travel all the way from Britain, on the western edge of the empire, to Cappadocia, on the eastern front.

At this time the entire Roman army consisted of twenty-eight legions, the toughest of which were stationed in the Danube region, on the northern frontier. There had already been signs of trouble in northern provinces, and even some recent incursions. Marcus nevertheless transferred tens of thousands of soldiers to the East from the Danube frontier, leaving it in a perilous condition. Governors in the north were ordered to use diplomacy to avoid conflict at all costs, or at least to forestall it until the Parthian crisis could be resolved.

Rome had two provincial armies in the East, each composed of several legions, which Marcus planned to deploy on two different fronts. First, the Exercitus Cappadocicus, or Cappadocian army, under the command of Statius Priscus, would retake the capital of Armenia. This army consisted of the two surviving Cappadocian legions, Legio XII Fulminata stationed in Melitene and XV Apollinaris from Satala, a third, unnamed legion having been lost by Severianus. These were reinforced by Legio V Macedonica from Troesmis (near present-day Brăila, Romania), under the legate Publius Martius Verus, Legio I Minervia from Bonna (now Bonn), under the legate Marcus Claudius Fronto, and vexillations (temporary detachments) from several other northern legions, under the command of Publius Julius Geminius Marcianus.

After the Cappadocian army had taken the Armenian capital, the Exercitus Syriacus (Syrian army), nominally led by Libo but under operational command of his legate Avidius Cassius, would drive the Parthians out of Syria and Upper Mesopotamia. Cassius originally commanded Legio III Gallica from Raphanaea but became responsible for also retraining Legio IV Scythica stationed at Zeugma and Legio XVI Flavia Firma from Samosata. The three Syrian legions were joined by Legio II Adiutrix from Aquincum (today's Budapest), commanded by Quintus Antistius Adventus. The two eastern armies each consisted of four legions, plus auxiliaries and vexillations. They must have numbered roughly eighty thousand men in total, supported by the Classis Syriaca, Rome's regional fleet. This was quite a large military force for Rome but well below the maximum that could have been fielded in an all-out war.

Near the beginning of the invasion, the Parthians tried to penetrate deeper into Syrian territory. Vologases had struck, believing the Roman garrison was still weak, but Avidius Cassius "made a noble stand," and his legions repelled the enemy.[19] The *Augustan History* contains a purported letter from Marcus to an unnamed prefect, possibly Lucius's traveling companion Furius Victorinus.[20] The two had been discussing Cassius, who had previously earned a reputation for strictness, even cruelty, as a commander on the Danube frontier. The prefect claimed that Rome's Syrian legions had become "Grecianized" and degenerate, loitering in the brothels of Daphne, and even bathing in warm water. Marcus describes Cassius as a man typical of the *gens Cassia,* a family known for upholding the "ancient discipline" of the Roman Republic. The prefect agreed that Cassius was the man to abolish warm baths and tear the flowers from soldiers' heads and necks. Marcus Aurelius had sent him east to restore discipline. It would prove to be the most ill-fated decision of the emperor's life.

CHAPTER TEN

The War of Lucius Verus

Lucius Verus embraced his co-emperor as they kissed each other good-bye. Although Lucius was his adoptive brother, he seemed more like a son to Marcus. Since he and Lucius were not alone, he leaned in close to whisper his advice: "When you have a banquet before you, remember to tell yourself that it is just a dead pig, a dead bird, and that the finest Falerian wine is merely grape juice and nothing more – by these and other means you must learn to moderate your desires."[1] At least we can imagine that Marcus might have said something of this sort. Lucius had heard these and other remedies for overindulgence many times. He enjoyed the advantages of wealth and status too much to practice temperance for long, though, when his Stoic brother was not there to supervise. Marcus understood human nature and had a wealth of psychological advice to share, but he recognized that Lucius was not interested.

Having accompanied Lucius as far as the town of Capua, in Campania, Marcus found himself being recalled to Rome by the Senate. Lucius had left Rome for Syria in the summer of 162, a journey that could potentially be completed in seventeen days.

Marcus had accompanied him about a third of the distance along the Appian Way, which led to the Italian port of Brundisium (Brindisi), before they parted company. Lucius assured Marcus that he would hasten to the East. In reality, though, he was in no hurry to arrive at the war.

Marcus had been called back to Rome to deal with urgent matters. He may also have wanted to be with his wife and children. Around this time Faustina gave birth to another son, given the name originally borne by Marcus: Marcus Annius Verus. Lucius continued, meanwhile, with his retinue, reputedly hunting in the region of Apulia, and partying at several villas along the way. He had fallen dangerously ill by the time he reached the town of Canusium (modern-day Canosa). Marcus, who had just returned to Rome, was forced to leave once again and speed to his brother's side. Traveling by carriage would take him at least five days. His brother's condition must have seriously concerned him.

Lucius had had the misfortune to be born on the birthday of Emperor Nero, a tyrant who was vilified by Rome's elite. Marcus mentions his brother's birthday twin only once, to use him as an example of how certain men can degenerate into animals dominated by their appetites.[2] One early historian described Lucius as "a second Nero," except that he was neither cruel nor given to acting, the latter trait considered thoroughly disreputable by most Romans.[3] Lucius, like Nero, was a nervous speaker, a binge drinker, and a gambling addict who enjoyed an extravagant and indulgent lifestyle. In addition to his other excesses, en route to Syria he became notorious for his adulterous relationships with women and affairs with young men.[4]

The *Augustan History,* the main source for Lucius's life, describes him as neither one of the best emperors nor one of the worst; he exhibited a mixture of virtues and vices.[5] Yet for some reason its author chooses to dwell on Lucius's vices, depicting him as an irresponsible drunkard and a playboy. Most modern scholars feel that these tales of licentiousness are embellished.[6] Although the evidence against Lucius is sparse, it seems to me that other sources lend some credence to his portrayal—perhaps it is an exaggerated version of his real character traits. We are told that Lucius's moral principles were far more lax than Marcus's but that he was honest and utterly guileless. The only traits Marcus could find to praise in his brother were his loyalty and affection; he saw Lucius as lacking the wisdom upon which other virtues depend.[7] He comes across as a deeply flawed but relatively harmless individual, perhaps even a likable rogue.

Lucius might, however, have been an alcoholic. As soon as he was free of his brother's supervision, he began to drink so heavily that his physical and mental health deteriorated. Only after three days of bloodletting and fasting (that is, abstaining from wine) was Lucius fit to continue his journey. Fronto, however, was concerned that he might immediately relapse and begin binging again, and he wrote to him: "I pray and beseech you, my Lord, take heed, as befits your eminent character, to be sparing and temperate and restrained in all your desires which now, after the abstinence which you have practiced on a necessary occasion, must necessarily make themselves felt more keenly and more importunately than usual."[8] It was not only later historians, then, but also Fronto, a close family friend, who saw in Lucius a man prone to dangerous bouts of excess.

Once he was back on his feet, Lucius resumed his journey to Antioch, albeit taking a detour through Greece and visiting Corinth and Athens, where he stayed in the villa of Herodes Atticus. (Many years later, Herodes would explode in anger at Marcus, venting his resentment over the burden that Lucius and his entourage had

Marcus Aurelius

placed on his household during this visit.) When Lucius reached Asia Minor, he stopped at various towns along the coast, before arriving in Antioch in his own good time. It is not certain how long this journey took, but his behavior drew bitter disapproval from the *Augustan History*:

> For while a legate was being slain, while legions were being slaughtered, while Syria meditated revolt, and the East was being devastated, [Lucius] Verus was hunting in Apulia, traveling about through Athens and Corinth accompanied by orchestras and singers, and dallying through all the cities of Asia that bordered on the sea, and those cities of Pamphylia and Cilicia that were particularly notorious for their pleasure-resorts.[9]

Marcus had thought that travel might teach the irresponsible Lucius to manage his expenditures, and that his character might be improved by the rigors of military service and the horrors of war — that he might even "come to realize that he was an emperor" and start behaving like one.[10] At the least, Marcus hoped that if Lucius continued his debauchery, he would do so far from the gaze of Rome's citizens.

Whereas Lucius acted as though he was taking the war lightly, Marcus's letters to Fronto at the time complain of his own insomnia due to worry over the threat posed by Vologases. Fronto replied with a list of Roman military disasters that were turned into victories, trying to reassure Marcus that Rome's fortunes might yet improve despite initial setbacks.[11]

It was probably early 163 when Lucius finally arrived in Antioch, in order, nominally, to oversee the army's logistics. The gossip said, though, that let loose in Syria, he "gave himself wholly to riotous living."[12] Instead of setting a good example to the troops, he "lingered amid the debaucheries" of Antioch and the nearby pleasure resort of Daphne.[13] From the troops in Syria he learned a new vice, staying up all night gambling on the roll of dice. He continued to drink so heavily that he often had to be carried unconscious to bed by his servants.

Word spread that Lucius, in a manner reminiscent of Nero, would wander the taverns and brothels at night with his friends.[14] Despite trying to conceal his identity by dressing like a private citizen, even wearing a cheap felt hat called a *pileus* — the ancient equivalent of a baseball cap — he was easily recognizable. The rowdy group would throw heavy coins at the taverners' ceramic cups, smashing them for sport. Lucius often got into drunken brawls and would awake the next day with his face black and blue.

Marcus may have had his brother on his mind when he wrote in the *Meditations* about "those whom you have yourself known distracting themselves about idle things" because they were unsatisfied with life and lacked the wisdom, and strength of character, to realize their true potential.[15] When he was not banqueting, Lucius was at the gladiatorial games or chariot races. While in Syria, he missed going to the Circus Maximus so badly that he frequently exchanged letters with friends in Rome discussing the chariot-racing results there. Before leaving Rome, he had courted controversy by becoming a patron of one of the two main teams. Lucius favored the Greens, like Nero before him, and donated large sums of money to them. This outraged the supporters of the Blues, their rivals. Lucius even took a golden statue with him everywhere he traveled depicting Volucer (Flyer), his favorite charioteering horse. In Rome, he pampered the animal with treats and brought it into the palace dressed in an imperial purple blanket, perhaps suggesting that he had bought the horse from its owner. When the horse died, Lucius had it entombed on the Vatican Hill and commissioned a costly crystal wine goblet named in Volucer's honor. The "Flyer" was a vessel so capacious that no man could hope to down its contents, and perhaps attempting to do so was a drinking game Lucius had invented.

After his lengthy journey to Syria, Lucius did not spend much time at his military headquarters in Antioch. In the summer he could often be found in the entertainment district of Daphne, and over the winter, when campaigning paused, he stayed in the nearby city of Laodicea. Indeed, shortly after arriving in the East he delegated command of the Syrian army to Cassius, apparently sidelining Libo, the governor of Syria. Libo had been sent east specifically to keep an eye on Lucius and report back to Marcus. Before long, he started going above Lucius's head, and would request direct authorization from Marcus for his activities in the province. Lucius must have hated this interference, and he soon began to resent Libo's presence.

CHAPTER ELEVEN

Parthicus Maximus

Marcus Aurelius listened in silence as Statius Priscus described the tactics required to wage war against the Parthians. Priscus was a decorated veteran of Hadrian's brutal war in Judaea following the Bar Kokhba revolt. He had since been trusted with one senior military post after another. The emperor, like Antoninus before him, was known for having the humility to give experts their due. "I should no more be ashamed to receive assistance," he wrote, "than a wounded soldier being helped up by his comrades in order to storm the battlements of a fortress."[1] Marcus intended to avoid repeating Severianus's mistakes, which had cost an entire legion in Armenia.

The general kept it simple. Over two centuries, he explained, since the massacre at Carrhae, they had learned the hard way about fighting the Parthians. Never stray far from sources of water. Stick by the rivers and hills, and avoid engaging their horsemen out on the plains, where they can encircle your infantry. He showed Marcus how Roman legionaries could be trained to withstand even a heavy cavalry charge by dropping to one knee, their javelins thrust into the ground like pikes. Priscus also stressed the need for ranged weapons. Slingers, though less accurate than archers, could harass the mounted enemy from a distance. This provided the covering fire essential for Roman cavalry to surround fleeing Parthian archers, while legionaries closed in for the kill.

Marcus, in any case, had chosen his general wisely. Once he arrived in the East, Priscus led the Cappadocian army with resounding success. He recaptured Artaxata, the capital of Armenia, in 163, and returned Rome's client king Sohaemus to the throne. The legionaries under his command boasted that their fearsome general had killed twenty-seven of the enemy with the sound of his war cry alone.

To commemorate Priscus's victory, Marcus and Lucius both adopted the title Imperator II, which meant that they were acclaimed emperors for the second time by the legions, a conventional mark of honor. Lucius also adopted the cognomen Armeniacus, "victor of Armenia." A letter of Fronto's makes it clear that Marcus was strongly opposed to accepting the same title and only relented a year later at his brother's insistence.[2] The Stoics had taught him to view with indifference the accolades awarded to him. Instead of placing value upon public titles, he should privately aspire to attain qualities like being "good" and "rational" in his own judgment, by consistently living up to those ideals.[3]

Around this time, however, the Syrian campaign experienced yet another unexpected, and possibly self-inflicted, setback. Lucius's second-in-command, Libo, suddenly dropped dead. As it was rumored that he had been going above Lucius's head and reporting concerns about his behavior to Marcus, Lucius was suspected of having him poisoned. Whatever the reason for Libo's mysterious demise, it must have disrupted the Roman campaign in Syria. Despite being a novice, Libo was the province's highest-ranking general. His post was temporarily filled by a hardened veteran, Gnaeus Julius Verus, who had decades of military experience. The Syrians, though, were quickly losing all respect for Lucius, and increasingly wished to be ruled by one of their own.

Following Rome's initial victory in Armenia, Lucius tried to negotiate terms with Vologases. The co-emperor was shocked when his attempts at diplomacy were sharply rebuffed by the Parthian king. He wrote to Fronto in distress, apologizing for not having contacted him earlier in the war. Lucius's excuse was that he did not wish to make his old friend "a partner in anxieties which night and day made me utterly wretched, and almost brought me to despair of success."[4] He explained that he had been "shackled with urgent cares," stressing that his plans changed daily because the outcome of the war seemed most uncertain. Clearly things were going seriously wrong.

The Parthians were adept at making tactical retreats. Most of their army was mounted, and well armored, allowing them to flee a losing battle before suffering many casualties. Two centuries earlier, Mark Antony had been dismayed to find, after routing thousands of Parthians, that only eighty enemy bodies lay on the battlefield. Likewise, despite Lucius's territorial victory in Armenia, Parthian troops in the region were still numerous enough to continue their campaign farther south.

Once driven from Armenia, enemy troops rode into the Roman client kingdom of Osroene, strategically located in Upper Mesopotamia between the Roman province of Syria and the Parthian Empire. The Parthians captured Edessa, Osroene's heavily fortified capital, perhaps aided by a faction within its walls, after the king, Ma'nu VIII, fled to the Romans rather than make a stand. Coins minted at this time show Vologases IV on one side and his newly appointed client king Wa'el on the other.

While the Parthians were occupied in Osroene, Lucius had taken as his mistress a beautiful and sophisticated young woman from Smyrna called Panthea. He even shaved off his beard to please her – an action the Antioch locals found risible. Much as Julius Caesar's and Mark Antony's associations with Cleopatra had been used against them in propaganda centuries earlier, the portrayal of Lucius and Panthea in the *Augustan History* seems designed to cast into question his competence to rule by insinuating that the emperor was under the thumb of a foreign seductress.[5]

In 164, Marcus's daughter Lucilla, who was betrothed to Lucius, turned fourteen. Marcus and Faustina set off with her for Syria, where the wedding was to take place. After briefly visiting his troops on the front line, Lucius departed to meet his bride-to-be en route. Allegedly, he did not want Marcus to witness his decadent lifestyle in Syria. Marcus, however, was forced to turn back at the port of Brundisium because he was needed urgently at Rome. Mother and daughter continued to the wedding.[6] Lucius and Lucilla were married in the city of Ephesus, in Asia Minor, halfway between Rome and Antioch. After her wedding, Lucilla was given the title Augusta. She was now, like her mother, Faustina, both the daughter of an emperor and the wife of one. At the age of fourteen, she had become the second-most powerful woman in the empire.

Avidius Cassius, meanwhile, had been preparing his legions to drive the Parthians out of eastern Syria and Upper Mesopotamia. The second phase of the war began in early 164, when he marched the Syrian army into Osroene to besiege the stronghold of Edessa. The Parthians had a tactical advantage on the steppe but struggled to hold cities when confronted with the advanced siege craft of Roman engineers. Cassius quickly took control of Edessa, perhaps aided by partisans within its walls.

The Parthians fell back to Nisibis, a heavily fortified frontier city, where an even more brutal siege followed. This was a turning point, mentioned several times by the satirist Lucian, who implies that the natives initially supported their Parthian occupiers but changed sides after an outbreak of disease.[7] When Nisibis fell, the routed Parthians fled down the Tigris. Their general, Chosrhoes, reputedly escaped by diving into the river and then hiding in a cave. When the Roman client Ma'nu VIII was later reinstated as king of Osroene, he publicized his allegiance by minting coins inscribed *Philoromaios*, "friend of Rome," bearing obverse portraits of the emperors Lucius and Marcus.

It was striking, nevertheless, that Osroene had fallen to the enemy *after* Lucius arrived in nearby Antioch. How could the gods allow a Roman emperor, the legions' priest and sacred representative, to be defeated by a "barbarian" nation? Although he had hastily assumed titles such as Armeniacus to commemorate his supposed conquests, Lucius never declared himself Osroenicus. If the recapture of Osroene was not celebrated, it was perhaps because Lucius did not want Roman citizens to be reminded that it had fallen on his watch. The local Syrians already saw this emperor as not only hopelessly dissolute but also a weak military leader who relied on his legates to run the war.

In the third phase of the counteroffensive, commencing in March 165, Cassius entered Upper Mesopotamia pursuing the remnants of the Parthian army downriver. Vologases was forced to retreat toward his capital, Ctesiphon, after he was deserted by his allies in eastern Syria and Osroene. Cassius fought his way past Dura-Europos, a wealthy and heavily fortified Parthian frontier city that guarded the Euphrates. As in previous campaigns, the Romans would have deployed ship-mounted catapults, and "terrible carnage" ensued during the siege.[8]

Cassius reached Lower Mesopotamia later the same year. His

army surrounded the twin Parthian cities of Ctesiphon and Seleucia, located on opposite banks of the Tigris. Seleucia, the former capital of the Seleucid Empire, had become rich from commerce along the Silk Road, and roughly half a million people lived there. Its inhabitants threw open their gates, welcoming the Romans as liberators. Establishing his base in this neighboring city made it easy for Cassius to besiege Ctesiphon, where the Parthian army now made its last stand. The enemy was soon routed, Ctesiphon was sacked, and Vologases's imperial palace razed to the ground.

Cassius's men did not stop, though. Their looting spread into neighboring Seleucia. According to some, the Seleucians had betrayed Cassius, although no details are given to justify what followed. Cassius's men sacked the entire city, burning it to the ground.[9] One source claims he took forty thousand inhabitants captive.[10] In an act that we would call a war crime today, and even Romans would consider unjust, he permitted his troops to turn on civilians who had surrendered and sworn allegiance to the emperor Marcus Aurelius.

During the looting, Cassius's soldiers broke into a temple of Apollo, seizing a precious statue of the god.[11] They also discovered a narrow crevice, which they broke through into a hidden shrine room.[12] Inside they found a golden casket, which they forced open, releasing a "pestilential vapor," which infected them, so the sources say, with a mysterious disease. The Antonine Plague was about to sweep across Marcus Aurelius's world like the mythic plague of evils set loose on the world when Pandora opened her jar. As Cassius marched his army back toward their base in Syria, dragging their loot and the precious statue of Apollo with them, famine and disease claimed many along the way.

When news of the Parthian capital's fall reached Antioch, the legionary commanders acclaimed Lucius and Marcus Imperator III.

Lucius also assumed the title Parthicus Maximus, "the greatest conqueror of the Parthians" — a rather grandiose claim, since Vologases, though weakened, remained in Parthia, commanding an army. Despite ceding most of Mesopotamia, he was not conquered. Nevertheless, "Lucius gloried in these exploits and took great pride in them."[13]

Lucius's gloating is confirmed by a letter in which he instructs Fronto to write a glowing history of his victories based on memoranda to be sent him from his generals Martius Verus and Avidius Cassius.[14] Lucius offers to supply Fronto with whatever details he requires on condition that the master rhetorician set his exploits in a flattering light. Fronto is to dwell on the early stage of the war, emphasizing the initial failures of Lucius's generals and the vast superiority of the Parthian army. This emphasis is necessary to highlight the greatness of Lucius's own achievements after his arrival at Antioch. As he was seeking to aggrandize himself at the expense of his generals, Lucius fails to mention that soon after he arrived in Syria, neighboring Osroene fell to the Parthians.

A draft preface from Fronto's *History of the Parthian War* was enclosed with one of his surviving letters.[15] It is very disappointing from a historical standpoint — full of tiresome literary clichés designed to flatter Lucius but telling us virtually nothing about the real events. A contemporary essay by Lucian, *How to Write History*, ridicules several pretentious, badly written accounts of the Parthian War.[16] Though he tactfully names no names, Lucian's criticisms could easily be applied to the propaganda piece on which Fronto was working.[17]

Cassius continued the counteroffensive in Parthia for at least another year, conquering the region known as Media, whose capital, Ecbatana, was another wealthy city on the Silk Road. Both emperors were acclaimed Imperator IV, denoting another key victory, and Marcus finally accepted the title Parthicus Maximus. Lucius claimed the additional title of Medicus, conqueror of the Medes. *Medicus* happens also to mean "physician" or "healer" in Latin, a coincidence that doubtless seemed ironic to those who later blamed Lucius for bringing the plague back from the East.[18]

In the Chinese annals of the Han dynasty is a record of ambassadors from a ruler named "An-toun" (Antoninus) arriving from Rome in 166. These records probably refer to Marcus Aurelius, who was often addressed as Antoninus in his official capacity as emperor; indeed, he calls himself that in the *Meditations*.[19] Travel from Rome to distant Serica (China), the land of silk manufacturing, though usually blocked by the Parthians, seems to have become possible for a brief period. Yet no mention of this embassy appears in Roman sources. The Parthians, whose wealth depended on control of the Silk Road, may have intercepted the ambassadors on their return journey.

Marcus could not hope to hold on to territory beyond the Euphrates for long, but the Parthians had at least been rendered incapable of launching another invasion. Martius Verus was placed in command of Cappadocia, and a well-trained army of veterans was now also garrisoned in neighboring Syria. Roman policy usually prohibited placing a general in command over his own homeland, yet Marcus made an exception for Cassius, installing him as governor of Syria. The emperor would come to regret leaving so many experienced soldiers, with no enemy to fight, under the command of a native general, especially one as ambitious as Cassius.

Roman citizens hated the concept of being ruled by a king, which they compared to slavery, but attitudes were different in the East. Lucius enjoyed the feeling of reigning over Rome's eastern provinces like an oriental monarch. One consequence of the Parthian War, moreover, was that at least militarily his reputation now outshone that of his brother, and the opportunity to bask in glory doubtless enticed him back to Rome.

Following his return, flushed with victory, Lucius was less inclined to restrain his excesses. He built a sumptuous villa on the Clodian Way, northwest of Rome, which became notorious for extravagant parties. Marcus turned a blind eye, although one banquet in particular drew criticism.[20] Lucius heaped presents on his friends, including exotic perfumes, priceless Alexandrine crystal goblets, and mule carriages with silver trappings. Guests were even invited to take home the handsome young slave boys serving them. The total cost was reportedly six million sesterces, a figure exceeding the annual salary of an entire legion. When Marcus learned about this debauch, his composure broke as he reputedly bewailed the fate of the empire. Whatever the reason, the spoils of the Parthian War did not appear to swell Rome's coffers for very long.

Marcus privately struggled to find qualities to admire in his brother. Despite his status as co-emperor, Lucius is virtually relegated to a footnote in the *Meditations*. Marcus writes that he has been motivated to improve his own character by Lucius's example – but does he mean an example to be *emulated* or one to be *avoided?* He mentions only Lucius's affection and loyalty, damning him with faint praise – perhaps there is even a hint of concern over rumors of Lucius's animosity and disloyalty.[21] I suspect that Lucius's flaws, though real, were amplified after his departure from Antioch by propaganda designed to whip up support for a would-be usurper. The emperors' main rival would show his hand soon, in the forthcoming civil war, but for the time being Lucius provided a softer target than his brother.

In October 166, Lucius and Marcus jointly celebrated their historic victory. It had been over two centuries since a Roman had marked a triumph over the Parthians. Both emperors received the title Pater Patriae, having chosen to defer acceptance until they had proven themselves in the Parthian War. Marcus's two surviving young sons, Marcus Annius Verus and Lucius Aelius Aurelius Commodus, were both given the title Caesar, although they were only three and five, respectively. The two Caesars were named after Marcus and Lucius, making it obvious they were intended to rule as co-emperors on the model established by their predecessors. Marcus had reservations, only agreeing to the arrangement at Lucius's insistence, and probably also at the behest of the Senate.[22] Marcus had long been in poor health and if he died his co-emperor would be left as sole emperor. Lucius was therefore making it clear to the public that he accepted his brother's sons as their rightful successors. The move would help refute gossip about him conspiring against Marcus, as well as making it harder for potential rivals to stake a claim to the throne.

The two emperors rode in a four-horse chariot behind the spoils of the Parthian War, including the statue of Apollo looted from Seleucia, which was later set up in the god's temple on the Palatine Hill.[23] Columns of Roman legionaries marched before them, followed by captured Parthian soldiers in chains. The Triumphal Route (*Via Triumphalis*) led to the statue of Jupiter Optimus Maximus on the Capitoline Hill. The emperors wore the *toga picta*, the purple ceremonial robe, their faces smeared with red paint, giving them the appearance of the god Jupiter, to whose temple they were headed.

Celebration of a triumph was the closest thing to deification a living man could receive in Roman society. Slaves standing behind the victors in the chariot would hold laurel crowns above their heads while whispering in their ears, "Remember you are mortal" (*memento mori*) and other phrases meant to stave off hubris. Marcus had never experienced this ritual before, but the words had a special meaning for him. He had studied the *Discourses* of Epictetus, who said that Stoics should emulate these slaves, with their memento mori, but apply it to human life in general: "that he whom you love is mortal, and that what you love is nothing of your own." Everything and everyone is temporary, according to Epictetus, and our dearest loved ones and most cherished possessions are merely on loan to us.[24]

The words of the triumphal slaves soon took on a more ominous significance, though. It was becoming clear that Lucius and his army had brought back more than loot and glory from the East. "It was his fate," some gossips said, "to bring a pestilence with him to whatever provinces he traversed on his return, and finally to Rome."[25] Even as Marcus Aurelius and Lucius Verus rode in triumph through the streets, an initial outbreak of plague had started to infect the city. The disease was spread far and wide by soldiers returning to their garrisons across the empire. Although Lucius celebrated his triumph over Parthia, the *History of the Parthian War* he had commissioned from his old friend and rhetoric master was never completed. Fronto died soon after, possibly an early victim of the plague.

CHAPTER TWELVE

The Antonine Plague

Every educated Roman knew how the *Iliad*, Homer's epic about the Trojan War, began. As punishment for dishonoring one of his priests, Apollo exacted terrible revenge upon the Greek armies: "He came down furious from the summits of Olympus, with his bow and his quiver upon his shoulder, and the arrows rattled on his back with the rage that trembled within him. He sat himself down away from the ships with a face as dark as night, and his silver bow rang death as he shot his arrow in the midst of them."[1] One soldier after another falls victim to a mysterious disease until bodies are burning all day long on pyres the length of the beach. Apollo, the god of healing, was also the god of plague.

Marcus Aurelius was just as powerless in the face of his own plague. The first outbreak affecting the city of Rome occurred in 166, shortly after the emperors had celebrated their triumph. On that day, the streets had swelled with roaring crowds who pressed forward to catch a glimpse of the shackled Parthians. Rome's supremacy was confirmed, its people were jubilant, and its emperors blessed. The moment, however, would be all too brief.

Soon an invisible army would march across the whole empire, laying siege to every town and city. Suddenly people everywhere were being struck down by a terrifying disease, as if the god Apollo meant to punish the emperors — but for what transgression? Enemies on Rome's borders were ready to pounce. Achilles had complained in the *Iliad* that the Greeks camped on the beaches of Troy were "being cut down by war and pestilence at once."[2] Marcus now faced the same double threat.

Many physicians were among the first to die, after being exposed to the infected patients in their care. Marcus would later contemplate this irony: "Think continually how many physicians are dead after often contracting their eyebrows over the sick."[3] Galen, one of the most celebrated physicians of antiquity, was in Rome to witness the initial outbreak. He was so alarmed that he immediately fled to the relative safety of Pergamum, his home city, in Asia Minor. As Galen was one of the fortunate ones, though, who turned out to be immune, he was able to study its victims closely. He became the empire's leading authority on what was sometimes even called "Galen's Plague" by later authors. Today, though, it is commonly known as the "Antonine Plague" after Marcus's imperial dynasty, the Antonines.

Although retrospective diagnosis is very uncertain, the most widely accepted modern hypothesis is that the Antonine Plague was caused by a variant of the smallpox virus. It spread wherever large numbers of people lived in close proximity. The major cities and legionary camps of the empire were the worst affected. Outbreaks seem to have occurred intermittently until Marcus's death, and perhaps for many years afterward, with mortality rates surging over the winter months.

Vomiting and malodorous breath were common symptoms — victims could be said to literally reek of the plague. Galen's patients suffered from internal ulcers, severe stomach pains, and diarrhea. If their feces turned black and fetid from internal bleeding, they would typically be dead within days. Roughly one-quarter of victims died; for the survivors, the disease tended to run its course within two or three weeks. Those who lived usually became immune to reinfection. If it was indeed a disease like smallpox, some may have been left visibly scarred, partially blind, or with permanent limb deformities.

The plague was most likely spread through coughing and sneezing. Galen described how, following initial flulike symptoms, the condition of his patients would deteriorate after the ninth or tenth day. They would develop a slight cough, which became more severe as the infection progressed; eventually they began coughing up blood due to ulceration of their windpipe. If the infection spread to their larynx, they often lost the ability to speak. At the same time, a horrific rash would spread over the body, usually erupting in clusters of raised pustules. These would often turn dark as blood congealed in them, covering the skin with rough scabs, and leaving the face and body in a hideous condition.

Millions of people died throughout the empire. The plague spread everywhere and "polluted everything with contagion and death, from the frontiers of Persia all the way to the Rhine and to Gaul." The fifth-century historian Orosius claimed that entire towns were depopulated as a result: "Everywhere country houses, fields, and towns were left without a tiller of the land or an inhabitant, and nothing remained but ruins and forests."[4] Those who survived and acquired immunity were asked to care for the latest victims, or help lay their bodies to rest. During the worst outbreaks, corpses were removed from the city by the cartload. Cremation of the dead was one basic measure believed to limit the spread of disease. Marcus ordered state funding to be allocated for the funerals of the needy.

He also ratified stringent new laws regulating burial. For instance, he prohibited the building of tombs above ground on country estates out of concern, presumably, that decaying bodies might further pollute the air with disease.

As ulcerations first appeared in the windpipe, physicians astutely deduced that sufferers were being infected through the air, which they desperately tried to purify by burning medicinal incense. This was, of course, futile. Affected cities and military encampments reeked of smoke and heavy fragrances such as myrrh. Over the course of the pandemic, Marcus observed the atmosphere change in the empire, both literally and figuratively, as the lingering threat of this ghastly disease became part of his daily life.

As physicians were powerless to prevent the horrors of the plague, the masses began turning toward religion and superstition. Propitiating the gods must have felt like their last hope. In the *Iliad*, the plague afflicting the Greek armies at Troy only relented when the appropriate sacrifices were offered to Apollo. Marcus, in his capacity as pontifex maximus, summoned foreign priests from across the empire to perform various arcane and exotic rituals of purification. Although he outwardly engaged in such ceremonies, in private he adopted a more philosophical attitude, viewing miracle workers with skepticism.[5] Marcus respected myths and rituals but saw them as symbols. He accepted the Stoic interpretation of such mysteries as expressing various aspects of a single, divine, universal Nature.

The *Meditations* was written during the plague, yet Marcus explicitly mentions it only once. The corruption of the air around us by pestilence, he says, pales in comparison to the corruption of men's souls by vice—he could have added that the two often go together.[6] Indeed, religious con artists had already started preying on the desperate and gullible. One charlatan planned to recruit a band of fanatics in order to plunder Rome. He gave regular speeches from the branches of a wild fig tree in the Campus Martius, prophesying that the world was about to be consumed by fire from the heavens.[7] One day, hoping to convince his followers that he could turn them into birds, which would escape the pestilence and looming apocalypse, he leapt from his tree and clumsily released a stork hidden beneath his robes. Nobody was fooled. He was tried before Marcus, who shrewdly pardoned him in exchange for a public confession.

Marcus appears to have been very tolerant of religious sects. It is sometimes claimed that he persecuted the Christians, although there is no compelling evidence of this. After reviewing the relevant criticisms, for instance, the classicist C. R. Haines concluded, "Marcus has been condemned as a persecutor of the Christians on purely circumstantial and quite insufficient grounds. The general testimony of contemporary Christian writers is against the supposition. So is the known character of Marcus."[8] As we have seen, Marcus was de facto co-emperor during most of Antoninus's rule, of which a later Christian commentator wrote: "Antoninus is admitted by all to have been noble and good, neither oppressive to the Christians nor severe to any of his other subjects; instead, he showed the Christians great respect and added to the honor in which Hadrian had been wont to hold them."[9] Two of the church fathers actually portray Marcus Aurelius as their defender. Tertullian, a contemporary of his, calls him a "protector" of Christians.[10] Irenaeus, the bishop of Lyon, writing toward the end of Marcus's life, likewise asserts that the Romans had given the world peace, and Christians traveled without fear wherever they went.[11] Aside from an account of Christians being persecuted at Lyon reported by Eusebius, written well over a hundred years after the alleged event and of extremely doubtful reliability, the main evidence typically cited against Marcus relates to the trial and execution of the Christian apologist Justin Martyr. This may well have occurred during the initial outbreak of the plague, when religious tensions ran high.[12]

Justin was born in Syria-Palestina, but after his conversion to Christianity, he wandered the East proselytizing, finally setting out for Rome during the rule of Antoninus. Later, during the urban prefecture of Junius Rusticus (162–167), when Marcus and Lucius were on the throne, Justin was brought to trial. The Romans required their subjects to honor the emperor and state religion by pouring a libation of wine before a shrine. They viewed refusal as evidence of sedition. Jews were exempt from performing such rites as they were permitted to follow their own ancestral traditions, whereas Christians often refused to follow either the Jewish or Roman tradition.

Imperial policy had generally been one of tolerance since the time of Trajan, who advised the governor of Bithynia and Pontus, Pliny the Younger, not to actively seek out Christians for prosecution. Justin and six of his followers, though, had been reported to the authorities for refusing to adhere to Roman customs. At the trial, Rusticus offered to pardon Justin if he would perform the libation voluntarily before the court. Justin refused, stating that it would be impiety for a Christian to sacrifice before idols. Rusticus then *ordered* him to comply, granting him a second opportunity to avoid the death penalty. Justin refused again, apparently saying that it was his wish, and that of his followers, to be martyred: "We are confident that if we are punished we shall be saved." Rusticus, in frustration, sentenced them to execution, as the law prescribed.[13]

Some readers today will consider this religious persecution. Most Romans viewed it differently. Justin had come to the city of his own volition, knowing that the law required him to honor the emperor, whose role included serving as high priest of the state religion. Rusticus offered Justin, more than once, a way to escape execution, but Justin told the court that he wished to become a religious martyr. This trial involved only seven individuals, moreover, not the large-scale persecution that is often envisaged. In the *Meditations*, Marcus reflects that voluntarily facing death can be wise and virtuous only when motivated by sound judgment, adding, "not from mere obstinacy, as with the Christians," in order to make a "tragic show."[14] Possibly he had Justin's martyrdom in mind.

CHAPTER THIRTEEN

The War of Many Nations

During the initial outbreaks of what would become a devastating plague, Marcus Aurelius turned his attention to another conflict, already brewing along the empire's northern frontier. Stifling a sigh, he patiently opened a letter from Alexander of Abonoteichus, priest of Glycon. In arcane language, the oracle pronounced that victory would be secured against the Marcomanni and Quadi, two prominent Germanic tribes, and peace restored only if the emperor sacrificed two lions, throwing them into the Danube along with sacred Indian herbs and flowers.[1]

Marcus privately viewed magicians with skepticism. Nevertheless, he ordered the ritual to be carried out. The lions swam to the opposite bank, where they were promptly clubbed to death by Germanic tribesmen, who reputedly mistook them for large dogs. It was not a good omen.

Marcus had been trying to keep a major war with the northern tribes in abeyance since early in his rule. Shortly after the outbreak of the Parthian War, in 161, when Rome was still recovering from flood and famine, a well-disciplined Germanic army fielded by the

Chatti breached the frontier defenses (*limes*) in Upper Germania and Raetia (modern-day Germany, Switzerland, and Austria). A new general had to be sent to the region to restore stability.

Farther east, a tribe of Sarmatians known as the Iazyges invaded Roman Dacia, wreaking havoc and killing the governor before being driven back. Threats across the northern frontier were ongoing, but while his troops were occupied in Parthia, Marcus had ordered his provincial governors to maintain peace at all costs through negotiation. With Rome now reeling from the outbreak of plague and recovering from a lengthy war in the East, the emperor faced an escalating threat along the northern frontier.

Around 166 a Germanic war party six thousand strong crossed the Danube, breaking through the border defenses and entering the Roman province of Upper Pannonia.[2] A band of Langobardi (Long-beards) and former allies of Rome called the Obii had seized the opportunity to attack while troops that were usually stationed nearby were still in Parthia. Even so, the invaders were quickly routed by the local garrison. Fearing Roman reprisals after this defeat, a delegation of envoys from eleven key Germanic tribes met with the governor of Upper Pannonia to sue for peace. Ballomar, chieftain of the Marcomanni, was appointed their spokesman, a move that suggested he was deemed responsible for the incursion.[3] (The Marcomanni were one of the largest and most warlike Germanic tribes; their name perhaps meant "Bordermen" since their territory seems to have reached the north bank of the Danube, bordering Pannonia.)

Most likely Ballomar had granted Langobardi and Obii warriors permission to camp in his territory, from which they launched their raid into Pannonia. They may have been mercenaries or vassals of the Marcomanni, or migrants displaced from their homeland by the encroachment of other tribes. The confederation of Germanic chieftains negotiated a treaty with the Romans, agreeing to stop cross-border raids in exchange for certain concessions. Ballomar swore an oath to keep the peace.

These initial skirmishes had been warning signs of a great onslaught, however, which was soon to come. The *Augustan History* claims that in addition to the warlike Marcomanni, other tribes, which "had been driven on by the more distant barbarians," threatened Rome.[4] They were prepared to attack Italy unless they were allowed to settle on land there. This movement foreshadowed the great migration of Goths and other Germanic tribes that began in the fourth century under pressure from the Huns and would ultimately lead to the fall of Rome.

In 167, not long after the peace delegation, Ballomar led a vast army of allied Germanic tribes into battle spearheaded by his Marcomanni warriors. The Quadi, the largest tribe in the region, were also persuaded to take part in the invasion. They had been among the Germanic tribes conquered under Antoninus.[5] A Roman coin dating from 140–144 CE inscribed *Rex Quadis Datus,* "a king is given to the Quadi," shows Antoninus crowning an unnamed Germanic ruler. Once they were defeated in battle, the Quadi surrendered and accepted a Roman ally as their king. They occupied the land along an important trade route known as the Amber Road, which brought precious gemstones and other goods from the Baltic coast through Upper Pannonia to Rome.

The Quadi were therefore wealthy compared to neighboring tribes that did not enjoy favorable relations with Rome. Their involvement in the uprising, which caught Marcus off guard, also brought many lesser tribes in their wake. For the Romans, this was a historic betrayal: in the *Meditations,* Marcus tells himself to maintain a philosophical attitude toward treachery and lies.[6] He recognized that both are part of life, as natural and inevitable as flowers blooming in the spring or the harvest of fruits in the summertime. Nonetheless, he and his co-emperor must have incurred criticism in Rome for trusting the word of Germanic chieftains, who had a reputation for breaking oaths.

According to the satirist Lucian, the Germanic "crisis" that followed began with a catastrophic Roman defeat, which has since become known as the Battle of Carnuntum. Carnuntum (near modern-day Vienna) was an affluent city situated in northern Pannonia at the intersection of two major trade routes, the River Danube and the Amber Road. It was therefore protected by an adjacent Roman fortress. Lucian claims that the Romans lost twenty thousand soldiers in a single day of fighting there.[7] These must have been largely auxiliaries and vexillations from nearby legions, perhaps sent to break a siege, as no evidence has been found of an entire legion being lost at this time, or, indeed, of Carnuntum having fallen into enemy hands. It is possible the Germanic tribes were so numerous they were able to overwhelm the provinces and surround Roman forts without breaching their defenses. Even so, the loss of so many men in a single battle would constitute Rome's most humiliating defeat of the war.

As soon as news of Ballomar's treachery reached Marcus, he began to make preparations for what was to become known as the Marcomannic War or, more accurately, the War of Many Nations. Marcus was, however, forced to delay because of the pandemic. He had been persuaded to officiate as pontifex maximus at an elaborate public ceremony called the *lectisternium*, described as a "feast of the gods."[8] Several sacred effigies, doubtless including that of Apollo, were placed on couches and honored with an extravagant banquet. This was meant to appease the anger of the gods and ward off the plague. Marcus hoped it would also appease the anxiety of his citizens.

After capturing Pannonia, Ballomar led his main army south, following the Amber Road through the provinces and into Italy, looting towns and enslaving captives along the way. Finally, they reached the wealthy city of Aquileia, which they surrounded.[9] A "barbarian" army had, to Marcus's dismay, marched across the Alps and invaded northern Italy for the first time since Hannibal, nearly four centuries earlier.

In the spring of 168, the two emperors rode forth from Rome, clad in the military cloak and boots. Before them went the Praetorian Guard, commanded by Furius Victorinus, who had distinguished himself serving under Lucius in the Parthian War. Marcus did not wish to send Lucius to the front alone this time and was afraid to leave him behind in the city "because of his debauchery." The decision for both emperors to go to war also signaled the gravity of the crisis in the North.[10]

The Marcomanni and their allies were "throwing everything into confusion," and the fighting was intense, with more Germanic tribes threatening to join them. It felt to residents of Rome as though the enemy were on their doorstep, although ten days' march remained between them. Marcus advanced into northern Italy with his Praetorians, joining forces with the legions for a major counteroffensive. The Germanic invaders, far from their homeland, were probably stretched thin at this point and running out of supplies. Despite their initial successes the Marcomanni lacked the siege craft and logistics required to take a fortified city, such as Aquileia, in the heartland of the empire. Nor were they prepared to face an imperial army at full strength in pitched battle. As Marcus approached, the invaders began their retreat back across the Alps, fearing they would be crushed by the huge force he had mobilized against them.[11]

Once the threat to Italy had been neutralized, Lucius spent all of his time hunting and feasting at Aquileia. Although Marcus took responsibility for military strategy, he appears to have delegated operational command of the army to Claudius Pompeianus, whose old friend and colleague Pertinax served as second-in-command. Before long, Marcus and Lucius were marching their army across the Alps to reinforce the legions in Pannonia, who were still fighting pockets of resistance from the Germanic tribes.

It was probably the first time Marcus had been outside Italy, and the first time either he or Lucius had been to the northern provinces. The roads were long and muddy, and the winters harsh. Marcus, whose health was already frail, struggled to project his voice enough in the frosty air to be heard by the troops. The emperors persevered and were jointly acclaimed Imperator V that year, as "a mighty struggle had taken place and a brilliant victory had been won," with the expulsion of the invaders.[12] Nevertheless, Marcus refused the soldiers' request for a donative, an indication that the public treasury was already nearing exhaustion despite the haul of Parthian gold displayed at Rome a couple of years earlier. Somehow he managed to avoid a mutiny and retained the loyalty of his troops.

Marcus immediately set up a new command, the Praetentura Italiae et Alpium (Border of Italy and the Alps), tasked with protecting northern Italy. Toward the end of the Parthian War, two entirely new legions, Legio II and Legio III Italica, had been formed. They were now placed under the command of a veteran of the Parthian War to help secure the Alpine passes.[13] Marcus's actions prove that he was extremely concerned in case the coalition of Germanic tribes might regroup and mount another invasion.

At the same time, the Romans faced mounting problems farther east from the Sarmatians. A nomadic warrior race descended from the Scythians, the Sarmatians were ethnically distinct from their

Germanic neighbors and were divided into various tribes spread across the Eurasian steppe. The most warlike, the Iazyges, controlled the territory sandwiched between the Roman provinces of Pannonia and Dacia. The Marcomannic invasion appears to have given the Iazyges an opportunity to intensify their raids in the provinces and perhaps to join forces with the Germanic tribes in their war against the Romans.

Marcus remained in Pannonia after the end of the campaigning season to receive embassies from the many smaller tribes that now surrendered. Some claimed to have put to death the instigators of the invasion, although Marcus was reluctant to take them at their word. Several tribes offered to fight on Rome's behalf.[14] The Quadi did not, but they did sue for peace, and sought Marcus's approval in replacing their fallen king, clearly wishing to recover their status as a Roman client state, and trading partner.

Marcus agreed to favorable terms in order to divide the Quadi from their cousins the Marcomanni. Indeed, the Quadi were made to swear that they would not allow Marcomanni or Iazyges to camp on or pass through their lands. They also offered to return deserters and Roman subjects captured during the invasion. Thirteen thousand prisoners were released in the first wave alone. The Quadi's right to attend Roman markets was not yet reinstated, however, because of concern that they might allow the Iazyges and Marcomanni to mingle among them and carry out reconnaissance on Roman positions while surreptitiously purchasing supplies. Although Stoicism taught kindness, this was to be tempered by prudence and caution. Marcus must often have been reminded of the Stoic teaching that, as in Aesop's fable of the farmer and the viper, acts of generosity are sometimes repaid with betrayal.[15]

With Pannonia largely free, the emperors returned across the Alps to spend the winter of 168–169 in Aquileia in anticipation of the campaigning season next spring. As the initial plague outbreak at Rome was abating, Marcus summoned Galen to his winter base to serve as court physician. On reaching Aquileia, however, Galen observed so many deaths there from the plague that he warned the emperors to return to Rome for their own safety.

One of the victims was Lucius's old companion, the Praetorian prefect Furius Victorinus. Shocked by the death of his friend, Lucius begged Marcus to accept the peace terms being offered by the other tribes and return to Rome. Marcus, however, refused to abandon the war. It seems that part of what he sought to achieve was the return of provincial Romans captured, and enslaved, during the invasion. To turn back now would mean forsaking tens of thousands of his own subjects being held behind enemy lines.

Marcus was astute enough to realize that his enemy was engaging in a strategy of deceit, feigning retreat and employing other "ruses which afford safety in war" in order to stall the Roman counteroffensive. The Germanic chieftains hoped that by tricking him into abandoning the war prematurely, they might launch another surprise incursion into Pannonia, and Marcus's army would be "overwhelmed by the mere burden of their vast preparations."[16] They were right about one thing: it was already evident that the imperial treasury was in danger of being exhausted by the war.

Lucius finally persuaded Marcus to return to Rome, leaving Pompeianus in charge of the campaign against the Marcomanni. While riding in the carriage beside Marcus, however, Lucius suffered a catastrophic seizure, which left him unable to speak. He died three days later at nearby Altinum. The cause of death may have been a stroke, but loss of consciousness and inability to speak could also be symptoms of the plague.

Marcus continued to Rome, as his brother had wished, although now bearing his corpse. Lucius had often frustrated Marcus, but they had grown up together and were obviously close. He had lost yet another person dear to him. Lucius was granted the honor of deification that had been denied his father. Although he was one of Rome's most popular emperors, beloved of the masses if not the senatorial class, no record exists of the date on which he passed away. It is generally estimated to be sometime in February 169.

Marcus Aurelius was now more isolated than ever, facing deception and treachery on all sides. Rumors circled about Lucius's sudden demise — some even claimed that Marcus had murdered him. This seems unlikely given that Marcus described him in his private notes as a loyal and affectionate brother.[17] It was Marcus who had insisted that the Senate appoint Lucius his co-emperor, who betrothed Lucius to his daughter, and who named one of his own sons after him. The younger, more vigorous emperor had always been expected to outlive his older, frailer sibling. Standing before the corpse of this man whom he had treated like a son must have filled the sole surviving emperor with a vivid awareness of his own mortality. Not long after this, Marcus began to immerse himself even more deeply in Stoic philosophy.

CHAPTER FOURTEEN

Germanicus

Trajan's Forum was crowded with visitors who had come to see Rome's elite display their support for the war effort, and find a bargain at the same time. Marcus Aurelius had ordered a public auction of imperial treasures, including palace furnishings, goblets of gold and precious crystal, and statues and paintings by famous artists.[1] A huge stash of jewels, conveniently discovered in a "holy cabinet" formerly owned by Hadrian, was also being auctioned. The empress Faustina had even been persuaded to donate a collection of silken, gold-embroidered dresses. Marcus pledged that once victory had been achieved the state would offer to buy back any purchases for the price paid, not unlike modern war bonds.

Marcus had grown indifferent to the luxuries of palace life; in this regard, he was a disciple of Antoninus, who had shown him that a man could live like a private citizen, despite being emperor, without the need for decorative robes, statues, and other trappings of wealth and power.[2] He reminded himself that for Stoics such treasures have no intrinsic worth. Even his purple imperial robes were merely sheep's wool dyed in the fermented innards of sea snails.[3] Privately, Marcus was relieved to empty the palace of so much clutter. He liked to recall a coarse joke made by the poet Menander about a rich fool with so many possessions that he has no room left to take a shit.[4]

The sack of Parthian cities had temporarily boosted the Roman treasury, until the impact of the plague and the cost of the Marcomannic War exhausted state funds. Lucius Verus's extravagant spending had not helped matters. Marcus did not wish to impose emergency taxes on the provinces, many of which had been suffering due to the recent military conflicts, and most of which were still afflicted by the plague. The auction continued for two months and appeared to raise enough money to help finance the rest of the war. (There may, of course, have been an element of political theater to it.) The country remained in the grip of economic crisis, however, and Marcus was forced to take radical steps, including debasing the currency. More coins were minted, although less bullion was available from which to make them.

The emperor had been levying fresh troops continuously for three years. He was now forced to adopt more desperate measures to replace soldiers who had been killed in battle or by disease.[5] First, he transferred to the army lightly armed patrolmen, called the Pursuers (*Diogmitae*), from some of the Greek cities. Marcus even recruited numerous bandits from Dalmatia and Dardania as auxiliaries, and hired Germanic tribesmen as mercenaries to fight against their neighbors. Next gladiators, who became known as the Compliant (*Obsequentes*), were enlisted. Finally, ordinary slaves, referred to as the Volunteers (*Voluntariae*), were invited to train for military service. Their conscription probably also included a grant of freedom, a risky and controversial measure. The Romans feared that, as in the notorious case of Spartacus and the Servile Wars, an army of slaves could turn against their former masters.

While in Rome, Marcus summoned Pompeianus to marry his daughter Lucilla, the widow of Lucius Verus, who, in addition to being the daughter of an emperor, remained an Augusta by virtue of her marriage. The choice of bridegroom was unpopular: Pompeianus was perceived by some as too foreign, too "advanced in years," and of too humble origin for Lucilla.[6] Moreover, the wedding took place within the official period of mourning for the deified Lucius Verus. Both Lucilla and her mother, Faustina, were opposed to this second marriage, but Marcus obviously felt the need to position Pompeianus as an alternative heir to Commodus, or more likely as a potential interim ruler. Perhaps crucially, marriage to Lucilla elevated Pompeianus in status above Rome's most senior general in the East, Avidius Cassius. The two men, both Syrians by birth, appear to have become bitter rivals.

Marcus had already proclaimed both his surviving sons, Marcus Annius Verus and Commodus, as Caesars. The younger son, Marcus's namesake, soon became his favorite. The historian Herodian even claims that the boy, like his father before him, was nicknamed Verissimus.[7] Shortly after Lucilla's wedding, however, the young Caesar died of complications arising during surgery on a tumor behind his ear. He was seven years old. Marcus later mused that while some men pray, "How shall I not lose my little son?" he himself should learn instead to pray, "How shall I not be afraid to lose him?"[8] He had counseled himself to recognize that the lives of our loved ones are, at least partly, in the hands of the gods.

Galen pleaded not to accompany Marcus back to the North and remained in Rome, attending to Commodus. The plague meant that the one surviving Caesar's welfare could not be guaranteed. Marcus therefore proposed to name his new son-in-law, Pompeianus, as Caesar, an action that would have given Marcus "an heir and a spare." Marcus wanted his son-in-law and general to mentor and one day rule alongside young Commodus. Pompeianus, though, declined the honor, possibly fearing that such news might provoke civil war in the East.

Marcus, able to spare only five days to mourn his son, left Rome to once again subdue the Marcomanni. The empire's frontier defenses were becoming increasingly vulnerable, and countless tribes joined the war, which now "surpassed any in the memory of man."[9] With one emperor dead and the other risking his life in Pannonia, wars also threatened to break out with the Britons and the Parthians, on the extreme western and eastern frontiers of the empire. In 170, moreover, another Sarmatian tribe, the Costoboci, rode all the way from their homeland near modern-day Romania through the Balkans and raided the Roman province of Achaea, all the way to the outskirts of Athens.

Marcus's old rhetoric tutor, Fronto, had passed away in the late 160s. Within a few years, his main Stoic mentor, Junius Rusticus, was also dead. Marcus was growing increasingly isolated, stationed far from Rome, and having lost so many friends during the wars and the plague. It must have been shortly after Rusticus's death that Marcus began writing the notes he titled simply "To Himself," which today we call the *Meditations*. No longer able to correspond with Rusticus about philosophy, Marcus now wrote to *himself* about philosophy. He became, in a sense, his own teacher.

From a number of internal references we can estimate the approximate date when the *Meditations* was written. Marcus describes Lucius, for example, as long dead. In one chapter's rubric, he notes that he is in Carnuntum, his main headquarters during the first phase of the Marcomannic War. In another, he records being across the Danube by the River Gran; this presumably occurred later in the war, as it places him in Quadi territory. Finally, no mention is made of the civil war, which broke out in spring 175, nor is there any indication that his wife, Faustina, has died (which happened later in 175); in fact, one note is a possible allusion to her being pregnant.[10] These and other pieces of textual evidence suggest that the *Meditations* was most likely written between late 169 and early 175, during the First Marcomannic War and the first few years of the Antonine Plague.

On his return to the northern frontier, Marcus campaigned against the Marcomanni, who had spearheaded the invasion of Italy. He suffered defeats early in the war and lost several senior officers. One Praetorian prefect having recently been lost, perhaps from plague, another was now slain in battle by the Marcomanni.[11] Initially, the enemy tribes had the advantage of greater familiarity with the terrain along the Danube frontier. One of the Roman army's greatest strengths, however, was its ability to adapt to different theaters and adversaries, and this flexibility slowly turned the tide of war in its favor.

Once the Quadi surrendered, the Romans marched across their lands to outflank the Marcomanni and pin them against the banks of the Danube. Marcus inflicted a crushing defeat on them, despite the plague having killed "thousands of [Roman] civilians and soldiers."[12] After about three years of intense fighting the Marcomanni were eventually defeated. We hear nothing more of their chieftain, Ballomar, who may have surrendered and was most likely sent into exile.

Around 172, the Roman client King Furtius, ruler of the Quadi, was overthrown by a chieftain hostile to Rome called Ariogaesus, presumably backed by the surviving Marcomanni chieftains.[13] Marcus had assumed that the threat posed by the Quadi had been eliminated after their surrender in 168. They now caught him off guard, though, by rebelling again. Although less warlike than their neighbors, the Quadi were a large and formidable tribe. Exhausted by fighting the Marcomanni, depleted by plague, and running out of money, the Romans were forced from one grueling war in Germania straight into another.

Two curious events marked turning points in the war against Ariogaesus. In the first, which became known as the Lightning Miracle, a Quadi siege tower was reputedly struck by lightning and destroyed after Marcus prayed for his men to be saved. Little more is known about this event, although it became famous, recorded by Roman historians and commemorated in sculpture and coinage. The coins show Marcus being crowned by the goddess Victory, which suggests that after the miracle the Romans won a major battle. It is quite possible that the more superstitious Germanic soldiers had simply been spooked by the impression that angry gods were warning them off with a lightning strike.

The second battlefield miracle, the Rain Miracle, was even more dramatic. It is recorded by a number of ancient writers, most notably the Byzantine scribe Xiphilinus.[14] This incident became important to Christians, who claimed that the legion involved included many soldiers sharing their faith. If true, this runs contrary to the charge that Marcus hated or persecuted Christians. A small detachment of a Roman legion commanded by Pertinax was facing certain death, having been surrounded by a much larger Quadi force. The legionaries had locked shields in a defensive circle. As no reinforcements were available, they were probably deep in enemy territory, perhaps near the land of the Cotini (modern-day Slovakia). The Quadi had them trapped in the open without water during a heatwave. The "barbarians" kept their distance, probably pelting the Romans with missiles, hoping to wear them down before breaking through their line.

Suddenly, to everyone's surprise, a heavy downpour began. The Romans caught water in their shields and helmets, drinking it down themselves and watering their horses. Seeing this, the Quadi charged, but the Romans fought and drank at the same time, gulping down water as it mixed with the blood of their wounds. As hail and lightning fell upon them, the Quadi were thrown into disarray, worried once again that the gods had turned against them. Pertinax and his men escaped with their lives, perhaps inflicting another major defeat on the Quadi at the same time. Ariogaesus later tried to negotiate peace, offering to return fifty thousand Roman subjects captured by the Quadi, but Marcus did not trust him, and refused to agree to terms.

Marcus Aurelius, a frail and bookish philosophy student, must have seemed an unlikely general at first. The fame of these miracles, however, suggests that his popularity was growing immensely with the troops under his command, who now saw their victorious Imperator as blessed by the gods. By this time, Marcus appears to have moved his base from the legionary fortress of Carnuntum farther east to Aquincum, close to the border between the Quadi and Sarmatian territory.

That the emperor refers in the *Meditations* to being across the Danube suggests that by around 172, Ariogaesus and the Quadi had surrendered and the Romans were beginning to secure their territory. Coins struck at this time declare Marcus Imperator VI and carry the inscription *Germania Subacta*, "Germania subjugated." By the end of the year, Marcus had also been acclaimed Germanicus, "conqueror of Germania." Indeed, a medallion struck the following year even announced his impending return to Rome. Finally, the war was over—or so it seemed.

CHAPTER FIFTEEN

Sarmaticus

M arcus looked out across the frozen surface of the River Danube, flanked by his two most senior generals, Pompeianus and Pertinax. The emperor tensed his grip on the reins of his horse as he watched a cohort of legionaries pursue a Sarmatian war party onto the ice. The Romans had learned to wait until enemy horsemen were returning from raids before attacking. "With this many slaves, and this much loot," Pompeianus explained, "they're as slow as infantry." Marcus knew as much already. "They're most vulnerable while recrossing the river," grunted Pertinax, "and our legionaries will be able to close in and surround them."

The Sarmatians had also adapted their tactics. They had concealed heavy cavalry in the woods across the river to ambush the Romans, who now marched out on the ice. Once the centurions gave the order to assume the hollow square formation (the standard defense against a cavalry charge) the legionaries would shuffle into position, forming four walls with their shields interlocked to protect the standard bearer (*signifer*) and lighter troops in the formation's interior. This usually worked when they were surrounded by enemy horsemen. The Sarmatians had discovered, though, that by charging hard across the ice and thrusting their lances powerfully enough into the wall of shields, they could knock the legionaries off their feet. The Romans were left slipping on the ice, thrown into disarray. Marcus would have heard his centurions bellowing the order "Keep in formation!" as the Sarmatian heavy lancers began charging thunderously toward them.

Having defeated the Germanic tribes, Marcus was on the verge of returning home when this new war had erupted with their Sarmatian neighbors. Around 173, he had moved his base of operations farther south, following the bend in the Danube, and stationed himself at Sirmium (in modern-day Serbia). Cassius Dio describes a great battle that probably took place in the winter of this year and signaled a turning point in the war.[1] Marcus's troops had developed a tactic to counter the Sarmatian ambushes. Now, legionaries on the frozen river formed the defensive square as usual. The soldiers on the inside, however, placed their shields on the ice, and steadied them in position. Their fellow soldiers on the outside then braced one heel against the shields to secure their footing.

This trick meant they could withstand a charge from heavy lancers even on ice and snow. With the enemy horsemen still reeling from their failed charge, the Romans could part their wall of shields for skirmishers to dash out and grab the reins of the horses, pulling them sideways, causing them to slip and fall. The Sarmatians were fearsome cavalry but no match for the Romans in close combat of this kind, and the frozen surface of the river was soon awash with blood, as the enemy, most of whom had been unmounted, found themselves in total disarray. Slipping on the ice and blood, unable either to fight or flee to safety, they were slaughtered in their thousands.

At about this time Marcus was acclaimed Imperator VII, indicating that the Iazyges had suffered a major defeat, perhaps this very battle on the frozen Danube. Banadaspus, their chieftain, tried to sue for peace, but Marcus refused. The Sarmatians had aided the Quadi rebellion and could no longer be trusted. Marcus's goal was presumably their unconditional surrender. When the other chiefs learned that Banadaspus had tried to negotiate with Rome they charged him with treason and replaced him with a more warlike ruler named Zanticus.

In one of the best-known passages of the *Meditations*, Marcus describes preparing himself each morning to adopt a philosophical attitude toward ungrateful, arrogant, and deceitful men.[2] He tells himself that such individuals are merely misguided: they have no conception of good. Furthermore, those who wrong him are fundamentally his kin. Not in terms of family ("seed") or even race ("blood"), to be sure, but because they share all humankind's capacity for reason, an even more fundamental bond. He tells himself that Nature intended us to work together, rather than fight, and that it would be irrational for him to feel hatred or anger for his enemies, or even to turn away from them in frustration. He was writing these words on the front lines of a bitter war, his mornings spent meeting the emissaries of hostile chieftains. It is remarkable to think of Marcus referring to the very "enemies" he is fighting as his brothers.

After two years of campaigning, the Romans were on the verge of defeating the Sarmatians. The empress Faustina came to Sirmium to join her husband, who gave her the title Mater Castrorum, "Mother of the Camp." (It is possible that she had been summoned in response to gossip spreading at Rome about her alleged infidelity, but her presence surely indicates Marcus's confidence that victory was at hand.) Zanticus now came in person to offer terms, which Marcus refused. The Iazyges allegedly still held captive over a hundred thousand Romans, "even after the many who had been sold, had died, or had escaped."[3] If this figure can be believed, it hints at the scale of the war and the vast number of mounted warriors the Iazyges must have been able to field. Marcus fought on, in part, because so many Romans captive behind enemy lines would not be freed until the Iazyges surrendered completely.

The *Augustan History* claims that by this stage, Marcus "wished to make a province of Marcomannia and likewise of Sarmatia," and that he was on the verge of doing so.[4] If such were the case, he was forced to abandon his goal — and his campaigns in the North — by a sudden and unexpected crisis in the East. Under a hurried agreement, signed without waiting for Senate approval, the Iazyges were granted the same terms as the Quadi and Marcomanni, possibly becoming Roman clients. They were required, however, to keep their distance from the Danube border because they still posed a threat of banditry. Marcus also agreed to terms securing the release of tens of thousands of prisoners captured during their raids. In addition, eight thousand Sarmatian knights were handed over to the emperor, who formed them into an elite cavalry unit. (Of these, fifty-five hundred were ultimately sent to distant Britain.) Marcus was acclaimed Imperator VIII and later took the title Sarmaticus, conqueror of the Sarmatians, indicating that the war was over. Maintaining the peace, though, brought its own challenges.

Even after enemies surrendered, the victors often had no guarantee they would keep to the terms agreed. The Quadi, for instance, had recently broken a truce, hoping to catch Rome off guard. Warriors captured in battle might simply resume fighting if allowed to return home. The Romans did not have prisoner-of-war camps. Captured hostiles were often auctioned as slaves, in order to neutralize them, but we find no mention of Marcus doing this. Instead, we are told he "scrupulously observed justice" even in dealing with enemy captives. Captured warriors from many of the smaller Germanic tribes were sent to fight in distant theaters; those who were unfit for battle were granted land in the provinces or even in northern Italy. The families of warriors who had joined Rome's auxiliary units were offered protection within the empire (although these could also be viewed as hostages).[5]

Having his conquered enemies beat their swords into plowshares was one way of disarming them, and it helped restore regions depopulated by the plague. Mass immigration, though, brought its own problems. During the Marcomannic War, perhaps after the Qaudi rebelled, Germanic settlers in Ravenna, in northern Italy, revolted and tried to seize control of the city.[6] The rebels may have been veterans who had returned to their families. After Marcus expelled them, he never placed foreigners in northern Italy again, although he did continue to settle them elsewhere in the empire.

Although Marcus was able to resettle many thousands of *Germanic* tribesmen with mixed success, the Sarmatians presented a new problem because of their nomadic lifestyle. They were proud horseback warriors who could never find a permanent home within the empire in such large numbers. Their raids on provincial towns were causing enormous trouble, and Marcus was unable to resettle them. The question then arises of why Marcus did not sell all of the captured Germanic and Sarmatian enemies to slave traders. An answer may perhaps be found in the attitude of Stoic philosophy toward slavery.

The *Meditations* contains many references to what might be called internal slavery, something all humans experience, insofar as they fall victim to irrational desires and emotions. The early Greek Stoics, who were fond of paradoxes, declared that true freedom consists in not being in thrall to unhealthy "passions" of this kind. The wise man can be free even if his physical body is clapped in irons. Evil men, by contrast, are all slaves, even if they appear to be powerful rulers. Marcus himself refers to Alexander the Great, Pompey, and Julius Caesar as slaves.[7] These men, he writes, annihilated whole cities, "cutting to pieces many ten thousands of cavalry and infantry" in battle, but because they were not wise, they sought wealth and glory at any cost. Their lives, in that sense, were tragedies of their own making.[8]

Marcus seems to have *physical* slavery in mind, though, when he says that hatred, war, and slavery day by day threaten his cherished moral principles.[9] Modern readers are often surprised to learn that some ancient thinkers considered the institution of slavery unjust. The New Testament, for instance, has little to say against it. The founders of Stoicism, however, considered owning slaves, whether acquired through conquest or purchase, morally wrong.[10] We can find fragments of a similar argument against slavery scattered throughout later Stoic texts, including the *Meditations*. This argument appears in its fullest form in a pair of orations, *On Slavery and Freedom,* parts I and II, written by a contemporary of Epictetus, the philosopher Dio Chrysostom.[11]

Dio, though a Sophist by profession, had studied under the famous Stoic teacher Musonius Rufus, and he later combined Stoicism with Cynicism and Platonism. He provides a simple argument to demonstrate the injustice of slavery. Following the Stoics, he distinguishes between slaves acquired through conquest and those acquired through purchase. Many people in the ancient world believed that certain "barbarian" races were *naturally* slaves. Dio, on the contrary, claims that as all men are born free, to capture and enslave them is to steal them from Nature, and such theft is therefore an unjust act — it is unethical, as we would say today.

Many slaves were born in bondage because their parents or

ancestors had been captured. All purchased slaves were likewise either stolen themselves or descended from those who were. All slavery, therefore, depended on the original injustice when "a man takes a prisoner in war or even in brigandage." "Consequently, if this method of gaining possession, from which all the others take their beginning, is not just, it is likely that no other one is either, and that the term 'slave' does not in reality correspond to the truth."[12] One person is called a slave if that person is *owned* by another but this is not true, as the enslaved individual has been stolen. In the same way that purchasing stolen goods is unjust, purchasing stolen people creates an "unjust" form of servitude — the institution of slavery is, in other words, immoral.

Marcus names the enemy he is fighting only once in the *Meditations*. What he says is reminiscent of the argument against slavery found in early Stoics and Dio Chrysostom. A person who takes pride in capturing Sarmatians, as though hunting hares and boars or catching fish in a net, has, Marcus says, the character of a brigand.[13] Humans are born free, and to enslave them is to steal them from Nature; since theft is unjust, only a brigand would take pride in it. The emperor must have owned slaves, although we seldom hear any mention of them. Nevertheless, Marcus's philosophical training evidently led him to question the ethics of slavery, and may even have influenced his actions.

Marcus appears to have sought alternatives to enslaving captured Germanic and Sarmatian tribesmen — as we have seen, resettling them within the empire or recruiting them into auxiliary units. Yet even if he did have concerns about the institution of slavery, he could not simply abolish it by decree. Rome's economy was based on slave labor, and threatening to overturn the status quo would risk civil war. We know that he believed in gradual political progress rather than revolution.[14] Did the Stoic emperor actually take any legislative steps, though, to improve the rights of slaves? Apparently, he did.

In response to a legal query put by his lifelong friend Aufidius Victorinus, Marcus gave a highly influential ruling that improved the rights of slaves to be manumitted. It is cited nearly twenty times in the surviving legal anthologies. Most often the citation is worded as "He attains his liberty in accordance with the ruling of the Deified Marcus," referred to as the "law of liberty," although the ruling is not quoted in full. The historian Anthony Birley concludes that despite the "harsh realities" of Rome's slave-labor economy: "It is fair to say that Marcus' attitude, as revealed not only by the much-quoted reply to Victorinus, but by other decisions made earlier in his reign, was one of deep compassion for the position of individual slaves, and that he did take some steps to improve their position."[15] Another scholar, Paul Noyen, carefully reviewed the Roman legal digests and identified more than three hundred references to texts by or about Marcus. More than half of these pertained to the rights of women, children, and slaves. Marcus wrote, for instance, the quite remarkable statement that it "would not be consistent with humanity to delay the enfranchisement of a slave for the sake of pecuniary gain." Noyen surely goes too far in claiming that these records show that "Marcus, faithful to his Stoic principles, aimed at the complete abolition of slavery."[16] Nevertheless, the emperor was clearly attempting to improve the rights of slaves gradually. For instance, he decreed that the law should set free any slave forced by his or her owner to make a false confession under torture. It is tempting to view his progressive attitude as a consequence of his legal advisers' belief in the Stoic doctrine of natural law and as foreshadowing the modern concept of human rights.

By this time, in the spring of 175, Marcus had been working for nearly a decade to stabilize the northern frontier through a combination of warfare and patient diplomacy. He had enacted controversial policies such as exiling foreign enemies instead of executing them, and resettling captured enemies within the empire's borders in order to disarm them. He had even proposed annexing Marcomannia and Sarmatia as provinces. He was forced to abandon his ambitious plans, though, when a courier arrived at Sirmium with the shocking news that his most senior general in the East, Avidius Cassius, was instigating an insurrection against him. Cassius had been acclaimed emperor by the Egyptian legion in Alexandria, adding its voice presumably to those of the legions in his native Syria. Cassius was also supported by a number of senators and other senior officials. Marcus Aurelius now faced a war against a powerful opposing faction within the borders of his own empire.

CHAPTER SIXTEEN

Cassius the Usurper

The capital of the Roman province of Egypt was an ancient Hellenistic city founded in the fourth century BCE by Alexander the Great, after whom it was named Alexandria. It was also his resting place, and his tomb there remained one of the most venerated shrines in the ancient world. Alexandria's citizens, the wealthy ruling elite, considered themselves ethnically distinct from the rural tribes who occupied the surrounding area. In order to understand the civil war that Marcus Aurelius faced, we must go back in time about three years, to an uprising instigated by a charismatic warrior-priest, renowned for his bravery, named Isidorus.[1] Isidorus led a tribe of nomads known as the Boukoloi (Herdsmen), who inhabited the marshlands of the Nile Delta region. They were probably struggling to maintain their livelihood, owing to the economic impact of the plague, increased taxation, and prolonged wars on the northern frontier. Whatever their frustrations were, these grew unchecked until they finally erupted in one of the most violent uprisings of Marcus's rule.

The rebellion began when several Boukoloi men disguised in

women's clothing tricked a centurion from Alexandria into believing they wished to hand over a ransom in gold for their captured husbands.[2] Instead they lured him into an ambush. They captured the centurion and his companion, who was ritually sacrificed, while the Boukoloi swore oaths, and, according to the account in Cassius Dio, devoured his entrails. The hostages freed from Alexandria must have been men of value to their tribe, most likely Boukoloi chieftains. They would now have the opportunity to exact revenge by leading war parties into battle against their former captors.

Small groups of mounted Boukoloi warriors began hit-and-run attacks on Alexandrian supply trains and patrols. Little by little, neighboring tribes joined the rebels until their numbers had swelled into a popular uprising. Raiding parties were probably composed mainly of horsemen and camel riders armed with wooden bows and spears, and lightly armored with cowskin shields. The Romans would probably have assumed they were facing a rabble, little more than bandits, without the capability to defeat a legion of professional soldiers in a pitched battle close to a major fortified city. When the insurgents massed outside the gates of Alexandria, however, its garrison was, most likely, far below full strength because of the plague. The Roman infantry lost the battle, perhaps overwhelmed by sheer numbers or lured into nearby wetland terrain where they would be vulnerable to ambush. The surviving legionaries were forced to retreat behind the city walls, where they remained trapped, gradually starving and dying of plague.

Alexandria was the second city of the empire, and known as its breadbasket, the biggest port from which grain was shipped to Rome. The Boukoloi's siege would have placed a stranglehold on crucial supplies. Marcus ordered Avidius Cassius to march his legions to Alexandria, break the siege, and relieve the garrison. This strategy, however, created a new problem for the emperor. Cassius, a Syrian-born noble, had spent his childhood in Alexandria during his father's tenure as Egypt's provincial governor. Cassius even named his own daughter Alexandria, as a reminder of his links with the region.[3] Marcus now risked having Cassius enter the city as a homecoming hero and leave with it under his dominion.

Yet despite the legions at his command, Cassius's victory was not assured, owing to the enemy's "desperation" and extraordinary numbers. Rather than meet all the tribes in open battle he sought to divide and conquer. We hear nothing of Isidorus's fate once his allies began to desert him, but it is known that Cassius defeated him and was proclaimed the savior of Roman Egypt. Marcus awarded the Egyptian legion, Legio II Traiana, the title Fortis, "Valiant," for standing firm while besieged. Cassius, meanwhile, left Alexandria in the care of an ally called Maecianus, who may have been his father-in-law, a famous jurist and at one time Marcus's legal tutor.[4]

Owing to its strategic and economic importance, Egypt was an imperial province, governed by a prefect of the equestrian class, directly accountable to the emperor. Most other provinces were governed by former consuls answerable to the Senate. Because senators held a higher social rank than equestrians, since the time of Augustus they had been permitted to enter Egypt only with the express permission of the emperor, for fear that they might try to exert influence over the prefect entrusted with the empire's breadbasket.

Cassius was a senator of consular rank. In order to march troops across Egypt's borders, he had to be granted *imperium,* supreme command over the province in the absence of the emperor, which also gave him authority over the Egyptian prefect and his legion. Cassius's influence in the East was thus beginning to exceed that of the former emperor, Lucius Verus, particularly in the eyes of ordinary soldiers. As Cassius had saved the lives of the besieged Egyptian legion, its soldiers would have considered themselves forever indebted to him. Even if his exceptional powers had been revoked once the crisis ended, the *personal* authority he acquired would have remained.

Cassius was now in position to challenge Marcus Aurelius, the incumbent emperor. He would have been able to study the route by which another usurper, more than a century earlier, had made his own way to the throne. After the death of Emperor Nero and a series of short-lived civil wars, Rome's most senior general stationed in the East, Vespasian, was acclaimed emperor by the Egyptian legion in Alexandria. He had earned considerable authority by putting down an uprising in Judaea, and the legions there and in neighboring areas under his jurisdiction were quick to declare their allegiance. Once he had secured control of the East, and the Egyptian grain supply, support for Vespasian's claim to the throne spread, his legionaries marched into Rome, and he seized the imperial throne. Following Vespasian's example, Cassius appears to have planned a similar coup.

Marcus had made the mistake of putting Cassius, who was born near Antioch, in charge of his birthplace. Cassius was, moreover, no ordinary Roman citizen. His mother, Julia Cassia Alexandra, was a Judaean princess, descended from King Herod the Great. His mother was also a direct descendant of Augustus, the founder of the Roman Empire, a fact doubtless used by Cassius to lay claim to the imperial throne. To cap it all, Julia was also descended from Cassius Longinus, one of the leading assassins of Julius Caesar. His royal pedigree combined with his authority over so many legions gave Cassius the appearance of an eastern monarch in the making. Moreover, the Cassian blood in his veins suggested to the Roman imagination that Avidius might be destined to slay another Caesar, the current emperor, Marcus Aurelius.

At some point, perhaps following the Egyptian uprising, while

Marcus was busy fighting the Quadi and Sarmatians, Cassius was granted an extraordinary command, with overarching authority (*imperium maius*) throughout the eastern empire, making him a kind of imperial viceroy.[5] He had been extending his authority since the end of the Parthian War eight years earlier, and was now one step away from his supreme goal. In the spring of 175, he returned to Alexandria, where he was acclaimed emperor by the Egyptian prefect and his legion. As emperor, therefore, Cassius now appointed his own Praetorian Guard.[6] In addition to Alexandria, support for his rebellion was strong in his Syrian homeland, and it soon spread to neighboring provinces. Cassius was both Rome's most senior general and an eastern dynast – he now became a rival emperor to Marcus Aurelius.

Cassius had allegedly received news that Marcus was dead, or perhaps that he was dying. Although Marcus would in fact live another five years, around this time he may have been alarmingly unwell; his health had been failing for some time, and symptoms of chest and stomach pain are described, along with insomnia, dizziness, and spitting blood. One Roman historian claims that immediately before the rebellion, Faustina, "seeing that her husband had fallen ill," became convinced there was no hope of Marcus's recovery.[7] A rumor spread that the empress, fearing her husband's imminent demise, had encouraged Cassius to seize power in order to protect her and her children, particularly Commodus, from rival pretenders to the throne. (As we'll see, though, Commodus apparently hated the rebels, and he condemned them as traitors.) Cassius, in any case, seized the opportunity to have himself acclaimed emperor, perhaps fearing that another contender might succeed Marcus, the most obvious candidate being his son-in-law, Pompeianus.

Pompeianus and Cassius, Marcus's two most senior generals, were born within a few years of each other, both of them in Syria.

Pompeianus, who was from Antioch, was of relatively humble stock, a member of the equestrian class, although he was adlected into the Senate by Antoninus Pius. When Marcus betrothed his daughter to Pompeianus, he effectively placed him second in line to the throne after Commodus. In addition to being married to an Augusta, Pompeianus had been made consul for the second time in 173, whereas Cassius had served as consul only once. Cassius was a nobleman, born for power, who must have felt gravely insulted at seeing a *novus homo* (new man), especially one from his own province, elevated above him.

The *Augustan History* contains a letter attributed to Cassius that, though of doubtful authenticity, nevertheless attributes further plausible motives to him.[8] The would-be usurper is shown complaining that Marcus Aurelius promotes men of humble origins, who are "eager for riches," ahead of nobles who believed status was theirs by birthright. The letter specifically singles out Bassaeus Rufus, a former senior centurion from an impoverished rural family, who had an impressive military career, culminating in his appointment as Marcus's Praetorian prefect. The same criticism would have applied, though, to Pompeianus, who had married an empress despite being the son of an equestrian. Marcus's other senior general in the northern campaign, Pompeianus's friend and righthand man Pertinax, would one day succeed Commodus as emperor despite being the son of a former slave. Marcus's meritocratic policies made sense when so many nobles were being lost to war and plague, but they clearly did not please the aristocracy.

Cassius, in this letter, also accuses Marcus of being too lenient, and calls for a return to the sterner, old-fashioned values of the republic: "Marcus [Aurelius] Antoninus philosophizes and meditates on first principles, and on souls and virtue and justice, and takes no thought for the state. There is need, rather, for many swords, as you see for yourself, and for much practical wisdom, in order that the state may return to its ancient ways."[9] Men like Cassius called for an abrupt end to the prolonged wars along the northern frontier through more violent means, such as the extermination of the Iazyges, a course that Marcus, had considered but did not pursue. Cassius and his faction on the Senate certainly did not want "the philosopher" to spend more time negotiating with their enemies. Marcus was by comparison a military dove, whose complex foreign policies were proving slow and costly. What he now faced was a rebellion led by Rome's most senior military hawks.

News of Cassius's secession reached Rome first. The Senate, in a knee-jerk reaction, seized his assets and declared him a public enemy – any man could now take Cassius's life with impunity.[10] The masses panicked, fearing that his rebel army might set sail from Egypt to sack Rome in revenge. Civil war presented a much graver threat to their safety than war on any frontier. We cannot know whether Cassius really believed in the claim that Marcus lay dying or dead. Perhaps he merely offered it as an excuse for having himself acclaimed emperor. Once his actions became known, the Senate sent him word that Marcus was both living and well. Rather than standing down, though, Cassius began preparations for a full-blown civil war.

CHAPTER SEVENTEEN

The Civil War

Marcus Aurelius must have raised an eyebrow, as he struggled to understand his new enemy's military strategy. "Cassius's rebellion has spread through the entire region south of the Taurus mountains," he read aloud from the letter sent by his general Martius Verus. From Egypt, through Syria and Cilicia, to the Cappadocian border, all the provinces in this region came under the extraordinary command that Marcus had formerly granted to Cassius. Cassius now had gone one step farther and claimed these provinces as his empire. "It doesn't make sense," Marcus said quietly. "That gives him control of seven legions at most." Pompeianus nodded: "Three in Syria, two in Syria-Palestina, one in Arabia, and one in Egypt." These legions were by no means the empire's finest. Three times as many remained loyal, including the hardened veterans of the Danube frontier. "Against such odds," wondered Marcus, "how could Cassius ever hope to win?"[1]

Pompeianus understood, though. "Imperator," he replied, "Martius Verus still commands the two legions, stationed north of the Taurus mountains, in Cappadocia, as you know." Marcus listened in silence, growing more concerned. "Their isolation from the rest of our army means that Cassius can field seven legions against the two who remain loyal to you in the East." Marcus knew that if the small Cappadocian army were forced to surrender, Cassius would have more legions at his disposal, significantly improving his chances of holding the eastern part of the empire.

The emperor also faced several logistical challenges. He could not easily move troops east to reinforce the Cappadocian legions. Although he was concerned about the city of Rome's safety, frontier troops loyal to him could easily reach it before Cassius's rebel army. The governor of Lower Pannonia had already been sent with special detachments to protect the empire's capital. However, this left fewer soldiers to defend the northern frontier. Even before the plague and the Marcomannic invasion, Rome had been able to spare only three full legions from the North, plus vexillations, for the Parthian War of Lucius Verus. A similar-sized expeditionary force would be easily defeated by Cassius's rebel army.

The Parthian War had effectively removed the "barbarian" threat at Cassius's back, freeing his troops to fight against other Romans. Marcus, by contrast, would have to leave most of his troops behind to defend the Rhine and Danube frontiers. Once the news about Cassius had arrived, moreover, it would take Marcus weeks to prepare his army for the counteroffensive, and another month to move it to the front. That delay would potentially give Cassius enough time to seize control of Cappadocia and its legions.

Marcus needed to find a large number of reinforcements and get them to Martius Verus in time. He knew of one race of warriors who could travel from the northern frontier to the East faster than anyone else: the Sarmatians. It was said of them that "they run over very great distances," whether in attack or retreat, "being mounted on swift and obedient horses, and leading one, or sometimes even two, to the end that an exchange may keep up the strength of their mounts and that their freshness may be renewed by alternate periods of rest."[2] By alternating mounts, the Iazyges, the main Sarmatian tribe whom Marcus had been fighting in the north, could reach Syria in roughly one-third of the time a Roman legion would take. This was the reason Marcus had hastily agreed to peace terms with Zanticus, the Iazyx chieftain, after the news of Cassius's rebellion reached him. Eight thousand Sarmatian horsemen were conscripted into a shock division roughly ten times the size of a normal cavalry unit. The "barbarians" whom Marcus had just been fighting would now form the vanguard in a war against his fellow Romans.

That these Sarmatian knights were sent to fight in the civil war is nowhere explicitly stated, although it is a reasonable inference.[3] A contemporary inscription states that Marcus sent one of his most senior cavalry prefects, with a massive auxiliary unit of Marcomanni, Quadi, and Naristi horsemen, "to punish the insurrection in the east."[4] It appears, therefore, that the emperor did send vast numbers of foreign cavalry racing ahead of his main army to reinforce the Cappadocian legions standing against Cassius.

The battlefield, though, was not the only place where Cassius posed a threat. Four decades earlier, as a teenager, Marcus had watched powerless while Emperor Hadrian raged against those he believed were plotting to seize his throne. Overthrowing Hadrian would have meant deposing his heirs as well, Antoninus and young Marcus Aurelius. Now Marcus's own heir, his fourteen-year-old son Commodus, found himself looking over his shoulder. Cassius was not acting alone: the rebellion included a faction of senators and senior military officers. Living amid panic and confusion at Rome, not knowing whom to trust, without his father there to protect him, young Commodus must have been anxious for his life.

Marcus ordered the young Caesar to travel to Sirmium, where he and his mother, Faustina, could be protected by the loyalist army. Commodus would be allocated key imperial powers to progressively secure his status as the next emperor. The *Augustan History* reproduces a letter, alleged to be from the Senate, insisting that Marcus begin the process of appointing Commodus his co-ruler for the sake of the empire's stability: "We ask lawful power for Commodus. Strengthen your offspring. Make our children free from care. No violence troubles righteous rule."[5] Commodus, however, was a boy Caesar of questionable character. Although the story seems implausible, it was rumored that a couple of years earlier he had ordered a slave to be burned alive in a furnace simply for running his bathwater too cold.[6] Once Marcus began granting him imperial powers, his character reportedly degenerated further, as he fell in with a bad crowd of hangers-on. Nevertheless, for most Romans, especially in the provinces, even a bad emperor was better than a full-blown civil war. Marcus either agreed with this sentiment or was oblivious to his son's flaws, for he now took steps to share the imperial power with him.[7]

At first Marcus tried to keep news of Cassius's secession quiet, as he planned his response. "Rumour, the swiftest of all evils," as the poet Virgil put it, spread throughout the camp, and the troops began to worry about the prospect of a civil war. Eventually, the emperor realized it was time to address the crisis in public. The text survives of an extraordinary speech, purportedly delivered to the army by Marcus Aurelius himself, and forwarded in writing to the Senate. The massed troops must have been astounded if he said anything like what is reported in this account.[8]

The emperor, addressing his "fellow soldiers," begins by apologizing for asking them to engage in war after war on his behalf, this time against their own kinsmen. Cassius, who used to be his "dearest friend," has been plotting against him, forcing them all into a military conflict detestable to the nation. Yet despite the enormity of Cassius's betrayal, Marcus argues in typical Stoic fashion, that there is no point bewailing his fate or becoming angry with the gods.

He then assures his troops that whatever personal danger he faces is of little concern to him, he is prepared to meet his own death with equanimity if needs be, "for I presume I was not born to be immortal." However, for Rome's sake, he wishes Cassius had presented his case for impeaching the emperor's authority, and laid claim to the throne, before a military or Senate hearing. Marcus could then have defended himself through rational debate instead of force of arms. He would even have stepped down voluntarily, "without a struggle," he claims, if it seemed to be in the empire's best interests. Having renounced his allegiance to the Senate and the people, though, and broken their trust, Cassius has made himself untrustworthy, effectively putting an end to any opportunity for senators to try his case legally.

The emperor goes on to say that the "Cilicians, Syrians, Jews, and Egyptians" forming Cassius's seven legions are not only inferior soldiers, their numbers are tens of thousands fewer than those of the soldiers remaining loyal. Despite Cassius's victories, Marcus asserts that his own troops should not be intimidated as "an eagle is not formidable when in command of an army of daws nor a lion when in command of fawns." It is these legionaries, most of whom sided with Marcus, not their former general, who fought and won the Parthian War. The commander of the Cappadocian army, Martius Verus, remains loyal, says Marcus, and he has achieved even greater victories than Cassius.

Marcus hopes Cassius might already have abandoned the rebellion on receiving news that he is still alive. He charitably assumes that Cassius had himself acclaimed emperor only because he mistakenly believed that Marcus was dead. If he has not ended the rebellion, he might yet stand down when he learns of the loyalist army marching against him. Marcus claims that his main concern is that he might be denied the chance to pardon Cassius if the latter takes his own life or is killed.

Finally, he voices a typical Stoic paradox. Win or lose, the only true benefit Romans could obtain from the current crisis would be to show the world that it is possible to respond with wisdom and virtue even to a civil war. This recalls a well-known passage in the *Meditations:* we should not consider apparent setbacks to be misfortunes but rather tell ourselves that to bear them well is good fortune.[9]

Some may question whether an emperor could have spoken about forgiving a betrayal on this scale – the end of the speech even includes the words "Perhaps all this seems incredible."[10] Would Marcus Aurelius in fact have been willing to appear before a Senate hearing and step down as emperor to prevent civil war? It may also seem unbelievable that he would offer, unconditionally, to pardon Cassius and the other rebels. Yet following the war, the emperor apparently kept his word, pardoning almost everyone involved.

Marcus wrote the *Meditations* before the civil war began. Even then he was anticipating betrayal. He tells himself to notice when he is offended by untrustworthy, shameless, or disreputable individuals. Yet a world without untrustworthy people is inconceivable, he notes, and it is foolish to demand the impossible from life. We will always encounter vicious people, and if we can accept this, we can respond to them wisely. He goes farther, placing the burden of responsibility squarely on his own shoulders: "But most of all when you blame a man as faithless or ungrateful, turn to yourself. For the fault is manifestly your own, whether you did trust that a man who had such a disposition would keep his promise, or when conferring your kindness you did not confer it absolutely, nor yet in such a way as to have received from your very act all the profit."[11] If he followed this advice, Marcus would have asked whether he had been right to trust Cassius with so much authority over the eastern provinces. Rather than being offended by his former friend's ingratitude, he would simply have reminded himself that the goal of life is to do what is wise and just without expecting anything in return.

After the war, Marcus would honor Martius Verus's legions: Legio XII Fulminata and Legio XV Apollinaris were granted the titles Certa Constans (Certainly Steadfast) and Pia Fidelis (Devoted and Loyal), respectively. Their unwavering loyalty, standing firm against Cassius's rebel army, halted the enemy's progress and gave the emperor time to deploy his auxiliaries. Although the Sarmatian and Germanic tribes had been at war with Rome only a few months earlier, huge units of their cavalry quickly arrived to reinforce Martius Verus on the eastern front.

The news that the emperor was offering to pardon everyone involved in the rebellion must have reached the enemy camp a few weeks later, while he was still marching toward them at the head of an army of seasoned veterans. Cassius continued to demand that his rebel army fight in what must increasingly have seemed like a suicide mission. Perhaps his men also felt they had taken up arms against their fellow Romans under false pretenses, misled by Cassius's unfounded claims of Marcus's death.

While Marcus was still on his way to the East, news reached him that Cassius had been killed by his own officers, bringing an abrupt end to a "dream of empire," which as Dio puts it, lasted only "three months and six days." The usurper was ambushed by a centurion who charged at him on horseback. His blow wounded

Cassius in the neck without killing him, but the centurion's accomplice, a junior cavalry officer, rushed forward to finish the job. The assassination may have been part of a coordinated effort: Cassius's Praetorian prefect was also put to death by soldiers, as was Maecianus, whom he had left in charge at Alexandria.

It is unlikely that the plot could have succeeded without the support of high-ranking rebel officers, although no mention is made of this in the sources. Marcus's extraordinary generosity toward Alexandria, the daughter of Cassius, and her husband, Druncianus, must have raised suspicions that they somehow helped to bring about the end of the rebellion.[12] Instead of being apprehended by Cassius's Praetorian Guards and executed for treason, for instance, the assassins were permitted to leave Syria carrying the usurper's severed head in a bag. They delivered it to Marcus, but the emperor refused to look at what remained of his former friend. He ordered them to give Cassius a proper burial. Nonetheless, he pardoned the assassins and honored his promise not to punish anyone else involved in the secession, thereby drawing a line under the civil war.

CHAPTER EIGHTEEN

The Setting Sun

Shortly after the civil war ended, Marcus Aurelius suffered another great loss. While traveling through Cappadocia near a village called Halala, the empress Faustina suddenly fell ill and died.[1] They had been approaching a pass in the Taurus mountains known as the Cilician Gates on their way into the region formerly controlled by the rebels. The sources are undecided as to whether she killed herself or died of a chronic illness.[2] If rumors were true, the empress may have feared documents would be uncovered implicating her in Cassius's conspiracy. Death at the age of forty-five was not unusual, though, for a Roman woman. Faustina had given birth to at least fourteen children, suffered from excruciating gout, and was enduring a long journey through harsh foreign terrain when she died.

Martius Verus succeeded Cassius as governor of Syria and was tasked with restoring order to the province. He reputedly burned Cassius's correspondence, so we will never know whether it included clandestine letters from the empress. Marcus, in any case, was devastated by his wife's death. He insisted that nobody involved in the rebellion should be executed, "as if in this fact alone he could find some consolation for her loss." Moreover, Dio claims that Marcus wrote to the Senate, "May it never happen that any one of you should be slain during my reign either by my vote or by yours. . . . If I do not obtain this request, I shall hasten to my death."[3]

Marcus appears virtually inconsolable in this letter. Yet he threatens to take his own life before allowing any of his former enemies to lose theirs. The Senate wanted to execute several of its own members for treason, presumably including some of the generals in charge of Cassius's seven legions. Senators complained that the "wickedness of [the conspirators'] rash course" deserved to be punished and warned the emperor that his leniency risked encouraging similar uprisings in the future. Unmoved by their protests, he stayed true to his Stoic values and kept his oath never to have a single senator executed.[4]

Marcus ordered those captured to be released "whether they were generals or heads of states or kings," implying that neighboring kingdoms, perhaps Osroene or Armenia, had joined the rebellion.[5] Calvisius Statianus, the Egyptian prefect whose legion had first acclaimed Cassius emperor, was banished to an island, but he was not beheaded. Marcus had all the evidence pertaining to his crimes burned.

These were men who, by joining the civil war, had taken up arms "both against him and against his son." Indeed, as Commodus was already Caesar, the rebels must have talked about deposing, exiling, and even beheading or otherwise executing him. Yet Dio believed that if Marcus had captured Cassius he would have spared him; he took measures to protect many others who conspired to "murder" not only Marcus but also Commodus.[6]

After Faustina's death, Marcus and his son continued their journey through the East. It was perhaps at this time that he visited the province of Syria-Palestina, formerly known as Judaea. The Jews had allegedly supported Cassius's rebellion, and Marcus is reported to have exclaimed, "O Marcomanni, Quadi, and Sarmatians, at last I have found a people more unruly than you!" Even so, he did not pass up a chance to benefit from their wise men: the Talmud claims that an emperor called Antoninus, most probably Marcus Aurelius, befriended the great rabbi Judah I and conducted lengthy philosophical discussions with him.[7] Some of these conversations appear to be rather folklorish and do not reflect what we know of Marcus from other sources. However, it was in keeping with his character to seek out the most learned men of the region, so the Talmud may contain a fictionalized account of real events.

Around this time Marcus also visited Egypt, where he conducted himself more like a private citizen and a philosopher than as a monarch, dressing in plain attire. Before continuing his tour of the provinces, he left one of his daughters at Alexandria, demonstrating his trust in the new prefect as well as his commitment to protecting the city. The final stop on his itinerary, "after he had settled affairs in the east," and en route back to Rome, was Athens. Dio states that "for the benefit of the whole world," Marcus "established teachers at Athens in every branch of knowledge, granting these teachers an annual salary." He personally appointed a chair of rhetoric and granted funding to chairs in philosophy, to be appointed by Herodes Atticus, for Stoicism, Platonism, Aristotelianism, and even Epicureanism—despite the latter school's traditional rivalry with the Stoics.[8]

Late in 176, Marcus returned to Rome, accompanied by Commodus. Crowds lined the streets. Marcus was older and frailer, he walked more slowly, he spoke less often and with greater difficulty. He had left Rome a bookish philosopher and now returned a gray-haired veteran general. He had witnessed the brutality of war up close for many years. In the *Meditations,* he refers to the grisly sight of severed hands, feet, and heads lying an unsettling distance from the rest of the body.⁹ He was known to have buried many of his own loved ones. The Roman people saw a man close to death, an extremity that added to his already solemn appearance.

Mounting the imperial Rostra, the emperor struggled to make himself heard above the cheering crowds. He was in the middle of talking about his many years' absence when the spectators began to cry out *Octo! Octo!,* holding up eight fingers each.¹⁰ He smiled at them, and agreed to distribute the generous sum of eight gold aurei per person for a celebratory banquet—roughly six months' wages. He canceled all debts owed to the state going back forty-five years, and had the related documents burned in the Forum.

In the aftermath of the civil war Marcus had granted Commodus the title Imperator. They now celebrated a joint triumph at Rome, and Commodus was given the tribunician power. The following year, 177, Commodus was made consul for the first time, despite his youth: he was only fifteen. Soon after he was granted the title Augustus. Although there may have already been warning signs behind closed doors, it appears that once the supreme power rested in his hands, Commodus's *public* behavior began to fall away from the high standard set by his father, through unnamed acts of immorality and cruelty.

The peace treaties negotiated with the northern tribes held for about two years; then another conflict erupted on the Danube frontier. So in 177, Marcus carried out the ancient rite of declaring war outside the Temple of Bellona, goddess of war, by throwing a bloody spear at a wooden post symbolizing the enemy territory. The *Augustan History* claims that he had become so famous for his love of philosophy that as he was setting out for the Second Marcomannic War, the people earnestly requested that he publish his "Precepts of Philosophy," as they were afraid that the frail philosopher-emperor might not return. Not only did he agree to do so, he also arranged a three-day public discussion of his book, the *Exhortations*. If this is true, it probably refers to something other than the text we call the *Meditations*, which seems unlikely to have been intended for publication. Another source, Aurelius Victor's history of the Caesars, likewise claims that Marcus was mobbed by a crowd of philosophers who pleaded with him to discuss "some difficult and very obscure points of the philosophical systems" before he left once again at the head of an army.[11]

Marcus rode north to deal first with the "Scythian situation" accompanied by his Praetorian prefect and a large expeditionary force; he defeated the Iazyges in a single, day-long pitched battle, and was acclaimed Imperator for the tenth time.[12] The Iazyges refused to agree to peace terms unless Marcus resumed his campaign against their Germanic neighbors, the Quadi, who had been allies but had now become "enemies dwelling at their doors."[13] Marcus once again engaged in extensive diplomatic negotiations with the northern tribes. Rome's alliance with the Iazyges grew stronger, and many of the restrictions placed on them after their defeat were relaxed. In order to maintain peace, the Romans had by this time garrisoned a huge force of twenty thousand colonial troops in temporary fortresses throughout the Marcomanni and Quadi territory.[14] The Quadi, objecting to this, attempted to migrate north into the lands of a neighboring Germanic tribe, but the Romans blocked their route, perhaps to keep them from rearming and beginning raids along the Amber Road.

Marcus's earlier plan to "make a province of Marcomannia and likewise of Sarmatia" had been interrupted by the civil war. When the Second Marcomannic War flared up in the North, he battled the Sarmatians, Marcomanni, Quadi, and their allies for three years, and, claims the *Augustan History,* "had he lived a year longer he would have made these regions provinces."[15] Cassius Dio likewise speculated that "if Marcus had lived longer, he would have subdued that entire region," transforming central Europe by incorporating modern-day Czechia, Slovakia, and eastern Hungary into the Roman Empire.[16]

In March 180, the aging emperor contracted the disease that would finally kill him – most likely the plague that is named after him. He immediately summoned his son to his bedside. Sources disagree on where this was – Aurelius Victor locates Marcus's place of death in the city of Vindobona (modern-day Vienna), whereas Tertullian places it in Sirmium.[17]

Commodus, fearing for his own life, pleaded with his father to abandon the war and return to Rome. Like Lucius Verus, he was desperate to escape exposure to the disease. Marcus warned Commodus that by leaving his post, he would risk being seen as a "traitor to the state."[18] When his son insisted, Marcus begged him to remain at least a few days longer; fleeing immediately would seem like cowardice. The emperor then abstained from food and drink in order to hasten his own demise.

On the sixth day of his illness, he summoned his friends and kinsmen to his bedside, expressing regret that he was leaving Commodus behind as sole ruler, for he now realized that his son was unsuited to power. This group probably included close companions such as his sons-in-law Pompeianus and Claudius Severus, his childhood friend Aufidius Victorinus, his Greek secretary Alexander Peloplaton, his Praetorian prefect Tarrutenius Paternus, and others. They were distraught at the sight of him, but he chided them, "Why do you weep for me, instead of thinking about the plague and about death which is the common lot of us all?" As they left he said, "If you now grant me leave to go, I bid you farewell and pass on before." They asked to whom he entrusted his son, and Marcus replied, "To you, if he prove worthy, and to the immortal gods." The army "lamented loudly" when they heard he was dying; they loved him alone, and had no faith in the co-emperor, Commodus.[19]

On the seventh day, and on the verge of death, Marcus would admit only Commodus to his presence. After a brief meeting, he sent his son away because his fear of being infected by the disease had mounted. The dying emperor then turned to the tribune of the night watch and gave him the countersign: "Go to the rising sun; I am already setting."[20] This phrase is in keeping with the many references in the *Meditations* to death as a natural process. It must also have sounded like a reference to the symbolism of Mithraism, the Mystery cult most popular with the Roman army. Mithras is typically depicted with two companions, Cautes and Cautopates, one holding up a freshly lit torch, the other holding one turned downward, as if he were extinguishing it on the ground. Together they symbolize the rising and setting sun.

Marcus Aurelius covered his head, as though going to sleep, and passed away quietly during the night of March 17, 180. He had ordered the Praetorians to guard his son, in order to scotch any rumors that Commodus was responsible for his death. Even so, Cassius Dio in his history insists that the emperor was killed by his own physicians, who wished to win Commodus's favor by hastening his transition to sole ruler.[21]

In Dio's opinion, Marcus's son was not evil but as "guileless as any man who ever lived."[22] He paints a picture of a naive and cowardly youth, easily manipulated by his companions, who slowly corrupted him, turning him into an increasingly self-indulgent and cruel man. These hangers-on persuaded Commodus to abandon the northern frontier for the high life back in Rome, leaving behind the many good men to whose care Marcus had entrusted him. The best Roman emperors maintained power by keeping the army and the Senate on their side; Commodus destroyed his reputation with both the moment he abandoned the northern frontier. Consequently, he was forced to hold on to power by turning himself into a kind of celebrity, putting on expensive games and making an exhibition of himself fighting rigged matches in the gladiatorial arena, in order to court public acclaim. This way of ruling invariably led to disaster.

Some historians claimed that Marcus hoped Commodus might die rather than become another emperor as tyrannical as Nero, Caligula, or Domitian.[23] Herodian notes that although Marcus had brought the best tutors from around the world to educate his son, he was concerned that Commodus, at eighteen, was still too young to command supreme power, and might be ruined by alcohol and debauchery. The Romans were inevitably reminded of Nero, who became emperor at the age of sixteen and quickly degenerated into a tyrant. "Nero had capped his crimes by murdering his mother," as Herodian puts it, "and had made himself ridiculous in the eyes of the people." Marcus was also concerned that foreign tribes on the Danube frontier, being "contemptuous of his son's youth," would use his own death as an excuse to revolt against Commodus.[24]

Cassius Dio was about twenty-five years old when Marcus Aurelius died, and he later served as a senator under Commodus. So he was in a privileged position to compare the two emperors, and his *Roman History* contains strong opinions on each man's rule:

> [Marcus Aurelius] did not meet with the good fortune that he de-
> served, for he was not strong in body and was involved in a multitude
> of troubles throughout practically his entire reign. But for my part, I
> admire him all the more for this very reason, that amid unusual and
> extraordinary difficulties he both survived himself and preserved the

empire. Just one thing prevented him from being completely happy, namely, that after rearing and educating his son in the best possible way he was vastly disappointed in him. . . . Our history now descends from a kingdom of gold to one of iron and rust, as affairs did for the Romans of that day.[25]

Even while Marcus was alive, Commodus resented some of his father's decisions. After abandoning the northern frontier, leaving Pompeianus, his brother-in-law and guardian, to handle the disorderly tribes, Commodus promptly reversed his father's orders by having the descendants of Avidius Cassius hunted down and burned alive as traitors, whether or not they had been involved in the rebellion. The most that can be said in favor of Commodus's rule was that it prevented another civil war from tearing the empire apart. Marcus Aurelius's real legacy can be found in the example set by his own conduct as emperor and in the influence of his surviving writings, known today as the *Meditations*.

Epilogue

THE HALL OF MYSTERIES

While the First Marcomannic War was raging, Marcus Aurelius, surrounded by death and betrayal, found consolation in writing his famous notes "to himself" on Stoic philosophy. He also made a solemn vow. If he survived long enough, he would go on pilgrimage to Athens and join the supplicants being initiated in the Temple of Demeter at nearby Eleusis. Hadrian had tried to bring the Eleusinian Mysteries to Rome, but their mystique was rooted in the Greek temple's ancient site.

During the war, a Sarmatian tribe called the Costoboci had looted the temple complex and destroyed its *telesterion*, or initiation hall. Marcus ordered it rebuilt. In his honor, the Athenians adorned the pediment of the Greater Propylaea (main gate) with a bust of the emperor, surrounded by poppy flowers, one of the symbols of Demeter, as they often grow in wheatfields.

The name of the goddess Demeter contains the suffix *-meter* (mother). She was everyone's mother, and visiting her temple in

Greece must have been a powerful reminder to Marcus of his own mother, Domitia Lucilla. It had been his dream to visit Athens ever since, as a young boy, he sat beside his sister on the end of his mother's bed listening entranced as Lucilla read from the Greek poets. Half a lifetime later, Marcus still quoted to himself the words of Homer, Hesiod, and Euripides.

Even as he worked on his philosophical notebook at Carnuntum, and later by the River Gran among the Quadi, Marcus's mind turned frequently to his own death—not the mere idea but the pressing reality, as he struggled for breath in the frigid Pannonian air and watched one human life after another disappear under the ground during the Antonine Plague and the War of Many Nations. By the time the civil war of Avidius Cassius broke out, Marcus had probably finished writing the *Meditations*.[1]

Immediately afterward, he traveled for the first time to Athens, the birthplace of Stoic philosophy. He was fluent in Greek, having studied it his entire life, but this was the first time Marcus had actually set foot in Greece and could breathe its air. He was now surrounded by native Greek orators and philosophers, immersed in the culture he had read so much about in books. He visited the Stoa Poikile, the famous colonnade where Stoicism originated, which looked out across the Agora toward the Acropolis. He would have seen the four giant frescos of historic and mythological battles on its walls from which the name of the "Painted Porch" derived.

The aging Sophist Herodes Atticus met him in Athens. Marcus asked his forgiveness for past disagreements, and invited Herodes to induct him into the Mysteries of Demeter: "For I made a vow, when the war began to blaze highest, that I too would be initiated, and I could wish that you yourself should initiate me into those rites."[2] Marcus later joined the thousands of initiates who gathered before the Stoa Poikile to hear the hierophant of Demeter open the annual ceremonies of the goddess, which continued for five days in Athens. After the initial ritual purifications, they would proceed by torchlight from Kerameikos, an ancient cemetery in the heart of Athens, along the Sacred Way to Eleusis, where a vast temple complex overlooking the Saronic Gulf hosted the Mystery cult of Demeter. Celebrations would continue for another four days before culminating with the initiation rites.

The content of the Mysteries was a state secret, and it was a criminal offense to publish anything revealing it. What we can say with confidence is that the rituals centered on the myth of Demeter, particularly the abduction by Hades of her daughter Persephone, who became his reluctant queen of the underworld. Demeter was also the goddess of grain and agriculture, and one of her main symbols is an ear of wheat or barley. Initiates drank a concoction known as the *kykeon* (mixture), believed to have been made from barley water and mint leaves. Some researchers have speculated that it may also have contained powerful psychotropic drugs, based on evidence of a deliberate cultivation and processing of ergot, a hallucinogenic fungus that grows naturally on barley and other crops.

The experience left initiates able "not only to live happily, but also to die with better hope," as Cicero puts it. Perhaps they felt they had expanded their consciousness and glimpsed a vision of the afterlife. Marcus entered the sanctuary unattended, ordering his Praetorian Guards to wait outside. He would swear before the hierophant that his hands were free of unlawful bloodshed, risking a terrible divine punishment if he dared lie. The emperor was making a public statement through this initiation. He underwent it in part "to prove that he was innocent of any wrongdoing," surely regarding the death of someone important, perhaps Faustina, Avidius Cassius, or even Lucius Verus.[3] He had originally pledged to undertake this initiation many years earlier, not long after the death of his adoptive brother.

Marcus had other reasons for participating in the ceremony. He was fascinated by religious symbolism. The Mysteries occupy a central place in Greek culture alongside philosophy. Major themes found in the *Meditations* clearly resonate with the myth of Demeter, such as accepting loss and even one's own death as processes of universal Nature. Socrates had said that those who engage in philosophy correctly study nothing but dying and being dead.[4] This training for death is one of the most prominent themes of the *Meditations*. Marcus returns many times to the Stoic maxim that our supreme goal should be to live in accord with Nature, which includes an acceptance of the transience of all material things, even our own lives.

The first-century CE Stoic teacher Cornutus left behind a text on Greek theology which explains that the name Demeter means "Earth Mother": the goddess of the Eleusinian Mysteries symbolized Nature and the earth. "It was with philosophical intent that they began to celebrate the 'mysteries' for her," he says; "mythology tells that she is first and last because the things that were born from the earth and sustained by it are dissolved into it; and this is also why the Greeks start and end their sacrifices with her." Along similar lines, Marcus tells himself that both death and birth are "mysteries" of Nature; life is composed of the elements, only to decompose and return to them once more – and such things being natural to us, they should not trouble us. Elsewhere, he quotes a passage from a lost tragedy of Euripides, which could hardly sound more Eleusinian: "Life must be reaped like the ripe ears of corn. One man is born; another dies." He loved this line so much that he repeated it later in the *Meditations*.[5] It foreshadows the watchword he gave as he lay dying: "Go to the rising sun; I am already setting." As grain is sown in the earth, and then reaped again: *one man is born; another dies*. Living, and dying, always, in accord with Nature.

Chronology

121	Marcus Aurelius born at Rome, April 26, named Marcus Annius Verus after his father
	Emperor Hadrian embarks on his first tour of the provinces
ca. 122	Annia Cornificia Faustina, Marcus's younger sister, born
ca. 124	Marcus's father dies of unknown causes
	Marcus's maternal great-grandfather, Lucius Catilius Severus, assists in his upbringing
	Marcus and his mother, Domitia Lucilla, move into the household of his paternal grandfather, who may have adopted him
ca. 125	Emperor Hadrian returns to Rome; gives young Marcus the nickname Verissimus
127	Marcus inducted into the equestrian order
128	Hadrian embarks on tour of Athens and eastern provinces, accompanied by Antinous
129	Marcus enrolled in the College of the Salii
130	Lucius Ceionius Commodus (Lucius Verus) born
132	Bar Kokhba uprising, leading to the Jewish War of Hadrian (132–136)
	Marcus introduced to philosophy by his Greek painting master Diognetus; attends public lectures by the Stoic teacher Apollonius of Chalcedon
ca. 133	Hadrian returns to Rome, where his mental and physical health begins to deteriorate
	Marcus and his mother leave his paternal grandfather's house
ca. 135	The empress Vibia Sabina dies
	Hadrian almost dies of a hemorrhage and becomes more aggressive toward his perceived enemies at Rome
136	Marcus takes the toga virilis, is betrothed to Ceionia Fabia, daughter of Lucius Ceionius Commodus, and is appointed prefect of the city for the Latin Festival

Chronology

Marcus begins his formal education in philosophy and rhetoric

Hadrian adopts Lucius Ceionius Commodus, renamed Lucius Aelius Caesar, as his successor

138   Lucius Aelius dies of a hemorrhage after consuming medicine; Hadrian adopts Antoninus as his new heir, naming him Caesar; Antoninus adopts Marcus and the young son of Lucius Aelius Caesar (later known as Lucius Verus), whom Hadrian also adopts as grandsons

Hadrian accuses Catilius Severus, Marcus's maternal great-grandfather, of plotting to seize the throne, strips him of his position as urban prefect

Hadrian dies, July 10; Antoninus acclaimed emperor

Antoninus annuls Marcus's betrothal to Ceionia Fabia, betroths him to his own daughter Faustina

Fronto appointed Marcus's Latin rhetoric tutor

139   Marcus serves as quaestor under Antoninus as consul

140   Marcus serves as consul, is named Caesar, Antoninus's official heir, and takes the name Marcus Aelius Aurelius Verus Caesar

Marcus appointed head of the equestrian order

Herodes Atticus appointed Marcus's main Greek rhetoric tutor

Death of Empress Faustina the Elder, Marcus's adoptive mother

145   Marcus appointed consul a second time; marries Faustina

Marcus makes first allusions to illness in letters to Fronto: chest pain and ulcers

146   Marcus expresses disillusionment with the study of rhetoric after reading Aristo

147   Faustina gives birth to a daughter, Domitia Faustina

Antoninus grants Marcus tribunician power, making him virtual co-emperor

149   Faustina gives birth to two sons, Titus Aurelius Antoninus and Tiberius Aelius Aurelius, who apparently die within the year

150   Faustina gives birth to another daughter, Annia Aurelia Galeria Lucilla

151   Daughter Domitia Faustina dies; Faustina gives birth to another daughter, Annia Galeria Aurelia Faustina

Chronology

152	Faustina gives birth to another son, Tiberius Aelius Antoninus, who dies some time before 156
	Cornificia, Marcus's sister, dies
ca. 155	Marcus's mother, Domitia Lucilla, dies
159	Faustina gives birth to another daughter, Fadilla
160	Faustina gives birth to another daughter, Cornificia
	Marcus and Lucius Verus serve as joint consuls
161	Antoninus Pius dies; Marcus and Lucius Verus acclaimed emperors, sharing power
	Marcus's daughter Annia Lucilla (age eleven) betrothed to Lucius Verus
	The Tiber floods, leading to famine and disease
	Faustina gives birth to twin boys, Titus Aurelius Fulvus Antoninus, who soon dies, and Lucius Aurelius Commodus Antoninus (Commodus), Marcus's only surviving son
	Vologases IV of Parthia invades Armenia, instigating the Parthian War
162	Lucius Verus departs from Rome to take command in the Parthian War
	Faustina gives birth to another son, Marcus Annius Verus
ca. 163	Lucius Verus arrives at Antioch; Armenian capital recaptured by the Roman general Statius Priscus
	Marcus and Lucius acclaimed Imperator II following victory in Armenia
	The Parthians invade the Roman client-state of Osroene and install their own king
	Lucius married to Marcus's daughter Lucilla in Ephesus
164	Roman forces recapture Edessa, the capital of Osroene, restoring their client king
165	Avidius Cassius leads the Syrian Army down the Euphrates, sacks the Parthian capital of Ctesiphon and its neighboring city Seleucia, on the Tigris
	Lucius and Marcus acclaimed Imperator III following victories in Parthia
	Avidius Cassius returns to Syria, losing many soldiers to plague and exhaustion

Chronology

166	Avidius Cassius's legions conquer Media and Babylon
	Marcus and Lucius jointly celebrate a triumph at Rome for the Parthian War, and are acclaimed Imperator IV
	Marcus's sons Commodus and Marcus Annius Verus both named Caesar, to rule jointly one day
	Avidius Cassius and Martius Verus, the leading generals in the Parthian War, appointed consuls
	Initial outbreak of plague at Rome
	Langobardi and Obii attack Pannonia but are repelled; King Ballomar of the Marcomanni leads a delegation of Germanic tribal leaders to make peace with Rome; on the frontier, Dacia is attacked by the Iazyges, who kill the provincial governor in battle
ca. 167	Ballomar leads the Marcomanni and a huge coalition of Germanic allies to invade the northern provinces
	Twenty thousand Roman soldiers lost in Battle of Carnuntum; Germanic tribes cross the Alps into northern Italy, besieging Aquileia
	Marcus plans to leave for the north but is delayed by the initial outbreak of plague
168	Marcus and Lucius leave Rome for Carnuntum
	The tribes sue for peace; expulsion of Germanic tribes from northern Italy and the provinces by Roman legions; Marcus and Lucius acclaimed Imperator V
169	Lucius Verus dies en route to Rome, possibly of plague; Marcus returns to Rome for the funeral and to raise funds and troops for the war
	Marcus betroths his daughter Lucilla to Claudius Pompeianus
	Marcus's son Marcus Annius Verus Caesar dies
	Marcus leaves for the northern frontier
ca. 170	Marcus probably begins writing the *Meditations*
	Faustina gives birth to her last known child, a daughter, Vibia Aurelia Sabina
171	Most of the invaders expelled from the northern provinces; Marcus stations himself at Carnuntum; many Germanic tribes sue for peace, and terms are made with the Quadi, dividing them from their former Marcomanni allies

Chronology

ca. 172	Marcomanni defeated; war resumes against the Quadi; Marcus moves his base to Aquincum
	Bucolic War begins; Isidorus and his tribal warriors defeat the Egyptian legion and besiege Alexandria; Cassius is granted imperium over the eastern provinces, defeats Isidorus
	Lightning and Rain Miracles occur during battles with the Quadi
173	Marcus acclaimed Imperator VI; moves south to Sirmium
174	Marcus acclaimed Imperator VII; Faustina named Mother of the Camp
	Iazyx chieftain Banadaspus sues for peace; Marcus rejects terms; Banadaspus overthrown by Zanticus, and the war continues
175	Marcus has probably finished writing the *Meditations*
	Marcus acclaimed Imperator VIII after the surrender of the Iazyges
	Avidius Cassius has himself acclaimed emperor in the East, triggering civil war; he is assassinated a few months later, ending the war
	Faustina dies en route with Marcus to the Cilician Gates
176	Commodus granted the tribunician power and imperium, becoming virtual co-emperor; Marcus and Commodus jointly celebrate a triumph at Rome for victory over the Germanic and Sarmatian tribes
177	Commodus appointed consul
	Second Marcomannic War begins
	Commodus marries Bruttia Crispina; is named Augustus, co-emperor
	Marcus and his Praetorian prefect defeat the Sarmatians; Marcus acclaimed Imperator IX
178	Marcus and Commodus return to Carnuntum to help quell the Quadi and other Germanic tribes
179	Marcus scores a major victory against combined Marcomanni and Quadi armies, acclaimed Imperator X
180	Marcus dies, March 17, at Vindobona or Sirmium, probably of plague; eighteen-year-old Commodus is left to rule as sole emperor

Genealogies

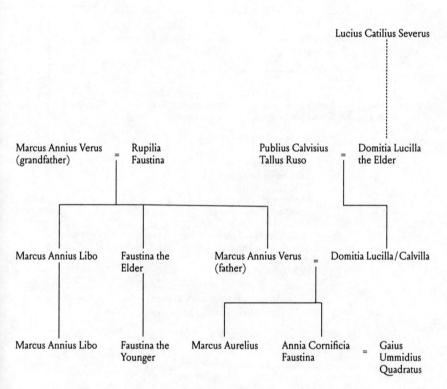

Lucius Catilius Severus

Marcus Annius Verus (grandfather) = Rupilia Faustina

Publius Calvisius Tallus Ruso = Domitia Lucilla the Elder

Marcus Annius Libo

Faustina the Elder

Marcus Annius Verus (father) = Domitia Lucilla / Calvilla

Marcus Annius Libo

Faustina the Younger

Marcus Aurelius

Annia Cornificia Faustina = Gaius Ummidius Quadratus

Birth Family
(dotted lines indicate adoptions)

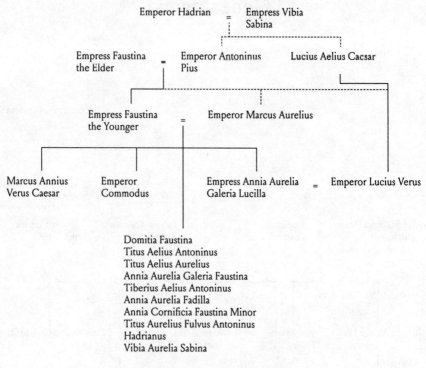

Emperor Hadrian = Empress Vibia Sabina

Empress Faustina the Elder - Emperor Antoninus Pius   Lucius Aelius Caesar

Empress Faustina the Younger = Emperor Marcus Aurelius

Marcus Annius Verus Caesar   Emperor Commodus   Empress Annia Aurelia Galeria Lucilla = Emperor Lucius Verus

Domitia Faustina
Titus Aelius Antoninus
Titus Aelius Aurelius
Annia Aurelia Galeria Faustina
Tiberius Aelius Antoninus
Annia Aurelia Fadilla
Annia Cornificia Faustina Minor
Titus Aurelius Fulvus Antoninus
Hadrianus
Vibia Aurelia Sabina

Adoptive Family and Children
(dotted lines indicate adoptions)

Source Notes

MEDITATIONS

The first printed edition of the Greek manuscript was published in 1558, edited by Wilhelm Xylander, and bearing the title *Ta eis heauton* ("To himself" or "Things to himself"). In 1634, the first English translation was published by Méric Casaubon under the title *Marcus Aurelius Antoninus the Roman Emperor, His Meditations Concerning Himselfe Treating of a Naturall Mans Happinesse; Wherein It Consisteth, and of the Meanes to Attaine unto It*. It has since been translated many times, though subsequent editions shorten the title to *The Meditations* or *Meditations*. Unless otherwise indicated, I have taken the quotation in this book from a modern version of George Long's 1862 translation (*Meditations: The Philosophy Classic*) with minor alterations in some places, noted as "modified." C. R. Haines's translation was published with the facing page Greek text in a Loeb edition. A. S. L. Farquharson's two-volume edition containing the text, translation, and commentary is another valuable resource. More recent translations, which are more accessible to modern readers, include the popular Gregory Hays edition, Robin Hard's translation, annotated by Christopher Gill, and Robin Waterfield's annotated translation, which is the latest one available at the time of writing.

CORRESPONDENCE OF FRONTO

In 1815, a cache of letters belonging to the rhetorician Marcus Cornelius Fronto was discovered by the Italian scholar Angelo Mai. They include letters Fronto wrote but also many letters addressed to him. The majority are between Fronto and Marcus Aurelius, his student, although there are also many between Fronto and other prominent individuals, including Domitia Lucilla, Antoninus Pius, Lucius Verus, and Avidius Cassius. These provide a direct window on Marcus's private life as Caesar and later as emperor. Although it is difficult to date the individual letters precisely, they span the period from around 138 to 166 CE. They include several essays, such as Fronto's so-called *Principia Historiae*, or *Preamble to a History* (of the Parthian War). Although the content, in a sense, is our most robust source for information about the life of Marcus Aurelius, it makes few references to historical events, and when it does, the information is often frustratingly vague. C. R. Haines translated the letters for the Loeb edition, which is the one I quote in this volume. The most recent translation, by Davenport and Manley (2013) consists of a selection.

Source Notes

HERODIAN'S *HISTORY OF THE EMPIRE FROM THE DEATH OF MARCUS*

Herodian of Antioch was a contemporary, approximately, of Cassius Dio, although an inferior historian, and probably a minor official in the Roman government. His *History of the Empire from the Death of Marcus*, written in Greek, takes Marcus Aurelius's death as his starting point, which limits the usefulness of his account for our purposes. Although he does add some color to the accounts in other sources, his reliability is uncertain.

THE CODE AND DIGEST OF JUSTINIAN

The legal compilations made by order of Emperor Justinian I preserve many rescripts and other pronouncements from Marcus Aurelius and Lucius Verus. Paul Noyen made the case that they reflect Marcus's Stoic beliefs ("Marcus Aurelius, the Greatest Practician of Stoicism"), whereas G. R. Stanton disputed this analysis ("Marcus Aurelius, Emperor and Philosopher"). Noyen claimed to identify references to 324 distinct legal texts either by Marcus himself or about his decisions, more than half of which specifically relate to women, children, or slaves, and generally tend toward improving their legal rights. Most of the references to children relate to the protection of orphans.

THE *ROMAN HISTORY* OF CASSIUS DIO

Cassius Dio, from Bithynia, was born into the senatorial class, and is believed to have been around twenty-five when Marcus Aurelius died. He wrote a history of Rome in eighty volumes of Greek, covering the period from its founding down to the time of Severus Alexander, whose reign began in 222 CE. However, the portion of the *Roman History* that deals with the life of Marcus Aurelius survives only in the abridged version, or "epitome," made by the Christian monk John Xiphilinus in the eleventh century. This is generally considered to be the most reliable written history of Marcus Aurelius's life, although it lacks a detailed account of the life before he assumed the throne. Of the volumes dealing with the emperor's early rule, and that of his predecessor Antoninus Pius, only short fragments survive. Dio held "Marcus Antoninus, the philosopher" in extremely high regard as an emperor, but clearly held a far different opinion of his son.

Dio had a ringside seat to Commodus's rule, as by this time he was a member of the Senate. However, historians are typically concerned that his obvious contempt for Commodus may have biased his retelling of events, and led him to exaggerate the latter's vices. The surviving material makes scant reference to Marcus Aurelius's brother and co-emperor, Lucius Verus. Sometimes it can be difficult to know what to make of the content. For example, Dio quotes at length from a remarkable speech that Marcus reportedly delivered to the northern legions upon the outbreak of a civil war. It provides a rare example of Marcus's own words in his official capacity as emperor, announcing political and military decisions showing traces, arguably, of Stoic philosophy's influence. Some have doubted its authenticity but Dio claims this speech was made in public, to the army, forwarded in writing to the Senate, and therefore probably circulated more widely.

THE *AUGUSTAN HISTORY*

The *Augustan History*, written in Latin, provides the most detailed biographical account of Marcus Aurelius. Its chapters on the lives of Hadrian, Aelius Caesar, Antoninus Pius, Lucius Verus, Avidius Cassius, Commodus, and Pertinax, and some passages in other chapters, also contain useful information about Marcus's life. The work purports to be by six different authors; the life of Marcus Aurelius is attributed to one Julius Capitolinus. However, modern scholarship has suggested that the entire history may be the work of a single author writing under several pseudonyms. It is addressed to the emperors Diocletian and Constantine I, who ruled from 284 to 305 and from 306 to 337, respectively. Modern scholarly consensus indicates a date of composition closer to the start of the fifth century CE.

It must be stressed that this text is notoriously problematic. It appears to contain a mixture of details derived from earlier historical sources and fabricated elements. Some of the letters and speeches are considered especially dubious. The work repeatedly claims, though, to be drawing on the lost biography of Marcus Aurelius written by Marius Maximus at the start of the third century, which is much closer to the period in question, although it may also be incorporating propaganda, gossip, or satire, alongside trustworthy historical details.

The Life of Marcus Aurelius is among the somewhat more reliable parts of the book. For instance, the men named as Marcus's philosophy tutors in the *Augustan History* are all mentioned by him in the *Meditations,* in a manner that appears consistent with this claim. The *Augustan History*'s comments about Marcus's legislative interests are also largely corroborated by the evidence found in Roman legal digests. Indeed, it contains many details that accord with information found in other sources. More caution is needed with regard to certain other parts of the text, often viewed with suspicion, especially the lives of Lucius Verus and Avidius Cassius, and some of the speeches and letters purportedly being quoted. Geoff Adams provides a recent analysis of the key chapters in *Marcus Aurelius in the Historia Augusta and Beyond,* which concludes "In general terms the HA will always be problematic, but it does provide historical value for us."

Notes

English titles are used throughout the text and notes. Classical works are cited by internal divisions only so that any translation may be used; the translations used in this volume are listed in the bibliography. Where I have made modifications to the translation, I indicate it with "modified."

ABBREVIATIONS

Amm. Marc.	Ammianus Marcellinus, *History* (*Res Gestae*)
Arr. *Epict. diss.*	Arrian, *Discourses of Epictetus* (*Epicteti dissertationes*)
Aur. Vict. *Caes.*	Aurelius Victor, *The Caesars* (*Liber De Caesaribus of Sextus Aurelius Victor*)
Cass. Dio	Cassius Dio, *Roman History* (*Historia Romana*)
Fronto, *Ep.*	Fronto, *Correspondence* (*Epistulae*)
Hdn.	Herodian, *History of the Roman Empire* (in Greek)
Luc. *Alex.*	Lucian, *Alexander the False Prophet* (in Greek)
Luc. *Hist. conscr.*	Lucian, *How to Write History* (in Greek)
M. Aur. *Med.*	Marcus Aurelius, *Meditations* (in Greek)
Philostr. *VS*	Philostratus, *Lives of the Sophists* (*Vitae sophistarum*)
SHA	*Augustan History* (*Scriptores Historiae Augustae/Historia Augusta*)
	Ael. — Aelius
	Ant. Pius — Antoninus Pius
	Avid. Cass. — Avidius Cassius
	Hadr. — Hadrian
	Marc. — Marcus Aurelius
	Verus — Lucius Verus

PROLOGUE

1. *SHA, Ant. Pius* 10.5.

2. Philostr. *VS* 2.1.8, modified.

3. Philostr. *VS* 2.9.3.

4. M. Aur. *Med.* 3.12.

5. M. Aur. *Med.* 9.1.

6. M. Aur. *Med.* 3.4.

7. "I advised you as to the preparatory studies necessary for the writing of history, since that was your desire," Fronto to Marcus Aurelius as Caesar, ? 139 A.D., sect. 8, Fronto, *Ep.*, vol. 1.

8. M. Aur. *Med.* 3.14.

9. M. Aur. *Med.* 6.53.

10. Compare the alleged criticism made of him by the usurper Avidius Cassius: "Marcus Antoninus philosophizes and meditates on first principles, and on souls and virtue and justice, and takes no thought for the state" (*SHA, Avid. Cass.* 14.5).

11. McLynn, *Marcus Aurelius*, 209.

12. See Robertson, *How to Think Like a Roman Emperor.*

13. The full title in Early Modern English is *Marcus Aurelius Antoninus the Roman Emperor, His Meditations Concerning Himselfe Treating of a Naturall Mans Happinesse; Wherein It Consisteth, and of the Meanes to Attaine unto It.*

14. M. Aur. *Med.* 1.17.

15. The *Augustan History* is a collection of biographies of Roman emperors and their heirs, purportedly written by several authors. See the Source Notes.

16. Everitt, *Hadrian and the Triumph of Rome*, xiii.

CHAPTER 1. THE MOTHER OF CAESAR

1. M. Aur. *Med.* 1.3.

2. M. Aur. *Med.* 7.59.

3. M. Aur. *Med.* 1.17.

4. Fronto to Marcus Aurelius, after August 13, 143 A.D., sect. 7, Fronto, *Ep.*, vol. 1.

5. See M. Aur. *Med.* 1.4.

6. Philostr. *VS* 2.5.4

7. M. Aur. *Med.* 1.11.

8. Romans 12:10, NKJV.

9. See Fronto to Lollianus Avitus, 157–161 A.D., Fronto, *Ep.*, vol. 1; Fronto to Lucius Verus, 163 A.D., sect. 6, Fronto, *Ep.*, vol. 2 .

10. Marcus Aurelius to Fronto, 143 A.D., sect. 2, Fronto, *Ep.*, vol. 1.

11. Fronto to Domitia Lucilla, 143 A.D., sect. 2, Fronto, *Ep.*, vol. 1.

12. Fronto to Domitia Lucilla, 143 A.D., sect. 3, Fronto, *Ep.*, vol. 1.

13. *SHA, Marc.* 1.9.

14. M. Aur. *Med.* 8.25.

15. M. Aur. *Med.* 1.2.

CHAPTER 2. VERISSIMUS THE PHILOSOPHER

1. *SHA, Marc.* 1.10.

2. M. Aur. *Med.* 9.21.

3. M. Aur. *Med.* 1.1, modified.

4. *SHA, Marc.* 4.1.

5. Livy, *History of Rome* 1.20.

6. See Virgil, *Aeneid* 8.285–302, for a description of the Salii and their hymn.

7. M. Aur. *Med.* 5.1.

8. M. Aur. *Med.* 7.61.

9. M. Aur. *Med.* 11.2.

10. *SHA, Hadr.* 15.10–13. Philostr. *VS* 1.8.1.

11. See M. Aur. *Med.* 1.5, where he is identified simply as "my tutor" (tropheus).

12. *SHA, Marc.* 1.10. We may perhaps see hints when this occurred as we are first told, here, that Hadrian gave the nickname to Marcus *after* his father died and, at *SHA, Marc.* 4.1, it seems to be implied that it was given *prior* to Marcus's induction into the equestrian order, suggesting that it was sometime between ages four and six that Marcus received the name Verissimus.

13. Cass. Dio 69.21.2.

14. M. Aur. *Med.* 8.30.

15. Justin, *Apology* 1.1. in Roberts, Donaldson, and Coxe, *Ante-Nicene Fathers.* Hdn. 1.2.1 also states that one of Marcus's sons bore the name Verissimus.

16. *SHA, Marc.* 2.1.

17. M. Aur. *Med.* 1.17.

18. *SHA, Marc.* 2.1.

CHAPTER 3. THE GREEK TRAINING

1. *SHA, Ant. Pius* 10.4.

2. M. Aur. *Med.* 1.6. Marcus mentions three men whose names, unfortunately, mean little to us today: Bacchius, Tandasis, and Marcianus.

3. M. Aur. *Med.* 1.6.

4. M. Aur. *Med.* 1.6, modified.

5. *SHA, Marc.* 2.6.

6. M. Aur. *Med.* 4.30.

7. *SHA, Marc.* 4.10.

8. *SHA, Marc.* 18.1.

9. Gellius, *Attic Nights* 19.12.10.

10. M Aur. *Med.* 1.16, modified.

11. See M. Aur. *Med.* 1.15, 1.14, 1.13, 1.9.

12. M. Aur. *Med.* 9.21.

CHAPTER 4. HADRIAN'S VENDETTAS

1. Aur. Vict. *Caes.* 14.6–9, trans. H. W. Bird.

2. *SHA, Hadr.* 14.8.

3. Apuleius, *Apologia* 1.11.

4. M. Aur. *Med.* 1.16, modified.

5. My intention here is simply to describe Roman sexual morality, without passing judgment on it from a modern perspective.

6. Birley, *Hadrian*, 241.

7. *SHA, Hadr.* 14.5.

8. Cass. Dio 11.3, 11.2 (citing Hadrian's autobiography).

9. *SHA, Hadr.* 14.6.

10. *SHA, Hadr.* 14.5–7.

11. *SHA, Hadr.* 14.11, my translation.

12. Aur. Vict. *Caes.* 14.6.

13. Marius Maximus quoted in *SHA, Hadr.* 20.3.

14. See Jones, "Aelius Aristides."

15. Jones, "Aelius Aristides," 151, 140.

16. Fronto to Marcus Aurelius, July 143 A.D., sect. 1, Fronto, *Ep.*, vol. 1.

17. I refer to Lucius Ceionius Commodus in this way to avoid confusion with his son, Lucius, and Marcus's son, Commodus.

18. *SHA, Marc.* 4.6.

19. *SHA, Hadr.* 15.5. Avidius Heliodorus was the father of Avidius Cassius, the usurper who instigated the civil war against Marcus Aurelius.

20. *SHA, Hadr.* 15.3.

21. Cass. Dio 69.4.1.

22. Cass. Dio 69.4.1.

23. Jones, "Aelius Aristides," 146.

24. Later, under Commodus, we are even told of the frumentarii carrying out assassinations at the emperor's behest.

25. Arr. *Epict. diss.* 4.13, trans. Oldfather.

26. Arr. *Epict. diss.* 3.4, trans. Oldfather.

27. *SHA, Hadr.* 11.6.

28. *SHA, Hadr.* 11.4.

29. *SHA, Hadr.* 4.1.

30. M. Aur. *Med.* 3.7.

31. *SHA, Ael.* 2.1.

32. *SHA, Hadr.* 23.11, my translation.

33. *SHA, Hadr.* 23.10.

34. Although "Caesar" had evolved into a title awarded to the emperor's chosen successor, it was also still a name retained by the emperor himself. For instance, the full regnal name of Marcus Aurelius was Imperator *Caesar* Marcus Aurelius Antoninus Augustus, so both the emperor and his heir could potentially be addressed as Caesar, depending on circumstances.

35. *SHA, Hadr.* 23.14.

36. *Virgil's Æneid,* 6.869–870.

37. *SHA, Hadr.* 11.3, modified.

38. *SHA, Hadr.* 11.3.

39. Aur. Vict. *Caes.* 14.8.

40. *SHA, Hadr.* 23.9.

41. Aur. Vict. *Caes.* 14.8. These accounts are not incompatible: she may have been forced to commit suicide by drinking poison.

42. *SHA, Hadr.* 23.7.

43. Cass. Dio 17.3.

44. *SHA, Avid. Cass.* 2.5.

45. Cass. Dio 17.2. The attribution of these words to Servianus was convenient for Cassius Dio's purposes as biographer. So we should be cautious about taking them literally, although the idea that Servianus might have expressed these feelings must have seemed plausible to Dio's readers.

46. Aur. Vict. *Caes.* 14.9.

CHAPTER 5. THE DEATH OF HADRIAN

1. *SHA, Hadr.* 26.9.

2. M. Aur. *Med.* 3.7.

3. *SHA, Ant. Pius* 2.1.

4. *SHA, Ael.* 7.2. Hadrian had said, "Let the Empire retain something of [Lucius Aelius] Verus," apparently insisting that Aelius's son should be adopted into the imperial family. Confusingly, the *Augustan History* attributes the cognomen Verus to Lucius Aelius Caesar, although this is not elsewhere attested and may be an error.

5. *SHA, Ael.* 7.3.

6. *SHA, Marc.* 16.6.

7. *SHA, Hadr.* 24.6.

8. *SHA, Hadr.* 15.7.

9. *SHA, Marc.* 5.3–4; M. Aur. *Med.* 1.11.

10. Hdn. 1.4.5.

11. *SHA, Marc.* 5.2.; Cass. Dio 72.36.1.

12. He references this image no less than seven times in *The Discourses*.

13. Arr. *Epict. diss.* 1.4, trans. Oldfather.

14. *SHA, Avid. Cass.* 1.8.

15. *SHA, Hadr.* 25.8.

16. Aur. Vict. *Caes.* 14.12.

17. Aur. Vict. *Caes.* 14.12.

18. Seneca, *Epistles* 51.

19. Cass. Dio 69.22.4.

20. *SHA, Hadr.* 25.7, 27.1

21. Cass. Dio 23.3; *SHA, Hadr.* 27.2.

22. *SHA, Ant. Pius* 2.3–8.

23. Aur. Vict. *Caes.* 14, trans H. W. Bird.

CHAPTER 6. DISCIPLE OF ANTONINUS

1. *SHA, Ant. Pius* 5.3.

2. M. Aur. *Med.* 1.16.

3. Jones, "Aelius Aristides," 146.

4. M. Aur. *Med.* 1.17.

5. M. Aur. *Med.* 1.17.

6. *SHA, Verus* 3.5.

7. M. Aur. *Med.* 1.11.

8. M. Aur. *Med.* 6.12, modified.

9. M. Aur. *Med.* 6.2–3.

10. See the praise of Antoninus at M. Aur. *Med.* 1.16.

11. See, e.g., M. Aur. *Med.* 6.30.

12. Fronto to Marcus Aurelius, ? 139 A.D., Fronto, *Ep.*, vol. 1.

13. M. Aur. *Med.* 6.48.

14. M. Aur. *Med.* 6.30.

15. *SHA, Marc.* 5.8.

16. M. Aur. *Med.* 1.17.

17. Much like the speech of Aristides, quoted earlier in this chapter.

18. M. Aur. *Med.* 6.30.

19. *SHA, Marc.* 2.4.

20. Cass. Dio 72.35.1.

21. Based on the evidence of his correspondence, modern scholars generally consider this praise overblown — though talented as a writer he does not seem to be in the same league as Cicero.

22. Marcus does mention Alexander the Grammarian, a lower-grade Greek-language tutor, and Alexander Peloplaton, who was indeed a Sophist but served as Marcus's Greek secretary, it seems, rather than his tutor.

23. M. Aur. *Med.* 1.17.

24. *SHA, Marc.* 2.7–3.3.

25. Cass. Dio 72.35.1. The manuscript actually names "Apollonius of Nicomedia," but this is generally agreed to refer to the man elsewhere called Apollonius of Chalcedon.

26. M. Aur. *Med.* 1.17.

27. M. Aur. *Med.* 1.13.

28. See To Herodes from Fronto, ? 144–145 A.D.; Fronto to Caesar, 145–147 A.D., Fronto, *Ep.*, vol. 1.

29. See Philostr. *VS* 2.1. Marcus is gently mocked for being an eternal student, and still going to the lectures of Sextus late in life. Sextus was the nephew of the famous Platonic philosopher Plutarch, and there is some uncertainty as to whether he was genuinely a Stoic as the *Augustan History* claims.

30. M. Aur. *Med.* 1.8.

31. *SHA, Marc.* 3.3.

CHAPTER 7. DISCIPLE OF RUSTICUS

1. M. Aur. *Med.* 7.19.

2. This is an imagined conversation drawing on M. Aur. *Med.* 4.41.

3. *SHA, Hadr.* 16.10.

4. Themistius, *Orations* 34, in Penella, *Private Orations of Themistius.*

5. Arr. *Epict. diss.* Preface, trans. Long.

6. M. Aur. *Med.* 1.7.

7. M. Aur. *Med.* 1.7.

8. Marcus to Fronto, ? 153–154 A.D., Fronto, *Ep.*, vol. 1.

9. On Eloquence 4, Fronto to Antoninus Augustus, ? 162 A.D., Fronto, *Ep.*, vol. 2.

10. Arr. *Epict. diss.* Preface, trans. Long.

11. Arr. *Epict. diss.* Preface, trans. Long.

12. Musonius quoted in Arr. *Epict. diss.* 3.23, from which the other quotes in this passage are derived, although slightly modified from the source.

13. M. Aur. *Med.* 1.7.

14. Freud himself studied psychotherapy in France under Hippolyte Bernheim and Jean-Martin Charcot and had other predecessors in the field going as far back as the middle of the nineteenth century.

15. See, for example, Plato, *Sophist* 230c–e.

16. M. Aur. *Med.* 5.28.

17. Arr. *Epict. Diss.* 4.5, 2.12, trans. Oldfather.

18. M. Aur. *Med.* 1.13.

19. M. Aur. *Med.* 6.30.

20. Marcus to Fronto, 145–147 A.D., Fronto, *Ep.*, vol. 1.

21. Fronto to Marcus, 145–147 A.D., Fronto, *Ep.*, vol. 1.

22. There is some disagreement among scholars about which Aristo Marcus Aurelius was reading. The philosophical nature of Marcus's anguish, though, suggests that it was probably Aristo of Chios. Aristo's works are lost now, but his teachings had been discussed at Rome, by both Cicero and Seneca.

23. Marcus Aurelius to Fronto, 145–147 A.D., Fronto, *Ep.*, vol. 1.

24. Fronto to Antoninus Augustus, 162 A.D., Fronto, *Ep.*, vol. 2.

CHAPTER 8. THE TWO EMPERORS

1. Paraphrase based on M. Aur. *Med.* 9.29.

2. M. Aur. *Med.* 1.14.

3. Antoninus's policy is an example of the Golden Rule in ethics that we find cropping up in the writings of Stoics. For instance, Seneca writes, "Treat your inferiors as you would be treated by your betters" (*Epistles* 47).

4. Cass. Dio 72.32.2.

5. The boys were all named after Antoninus, and the girls after Marcus's mother, Domitia Lucilla, and Faustina's mother, Faustina the Elder, who was also Marcus's adoptive mother.

6. M. Aur. *Med.* 1.17.

7. M. Aur. *Med.* 1.17, my translation.

8. *SHA, Ant. Pius* 13.3.

9. *SHA, Ant. Pius* 12.2.

10. The Antonine Wall is believed to have taken around twelve years to build but was abandoned around 158, only a few years after its completion.

11. *SHA, Ant. Pius* 9.10, quoting Scipio Africanus.

12. *SHA, Ant. Pius* 9.10.

13. *SHA, Marc.* 8.3.

14. Lucius had briefly been betrothed, years earlier, to Lucilla's mother, Faustina, now Marcus's wife.

15. Oddly, it appears that Lucius and Marcus became known as *Verus* and *Verissimus* respectively, or "True" and "Most True," which would surely make Lucius sound like a somewhat inferior version of his brother.

16. *SHA, Verus* 4.2.

17. *SHA, Verus* 3.7.

18. *SHA, Verus* 3.6.

19. *SHA, Verus* 10.6–7.

20. *SHA, Verus* 10.6.

21. Cass. Dio 71.1.3.

22. Emperors were acclaimed imperator (supreme commander) by the legions first, then confirmed by the Senate.

CHAPTER 9. THE PARTHIAN INVASION

1. *SHA, Ant. Pius* 12.7.

2. M. Aur. *Med.* 1.16.

3. M. Aur. *Med.* 4.49

4. *SHA, Ant. Pius* 9.6. See also Ross, *Roman Edessa*, 36.

5. *SHA, Ant. Pius* 9.6.

6. *SHA, Ant. Pius* 9.6. We are not told the date but it seems logical to assume Vologases' plans to invade Armenia came after his conquest of Characene.

7. *SHA, Marc.* 8.6.

8. For brevity, I shall generally refer to Marcus alone as emperor, although it should be taken as implied that he ruled jointly with Lucius Verus throughout this period.

9. See Plutarch's Life of Crassus in his *Lives,* and Peter Stothard, *Crassus: The First Tycoon* (New Haven: Yale University Press, 2022).

10. Fronto to Marcus Antoninus, 165 A.D., sect. 14, Fronto, *Ep.,* vol. 2.

11. The legendary comic book writer Alan Moore recently became a modern-day acolyte of Glycon, so he claims, after finding his statue endearing because he "looked so smug," with a head that reminded him of Paris Hilton.

12. Luc. *Hist. conscr.* 2.

13. At least, this seems to be what Lucian implies.

14. Some scholars believe this may explain the mystery of the lost Legio IX Hispana.

15. The presence of an emperor at the front brought more specific benefits – e.g., soldiers fought more bravely, supplies were more available, allies more supportive, and enemies more amenable to negotiation.

16. At times, the Praetorians were less reliable or competent soldiers, such as during the reign of Commodus. Under Marcus Aurelius, though, they appear to have won several major battles.

17. *SHA, Marc.* 20.2.

18. Our knowledge of the Parthian War, via the *Augustan History* and other ancient sources, probably derived ultimately from *commentarii* of the war written by Martius Verus and Avidius Cassius, mentioned in one of Lucius's letters to Fronto.

19. Cass. Dio 71.2.3.

20. *SHA, Avid. Cass.* 5.4.

CHAPTER 10. THE WAR OF LUCIUS VERUS

1. Based upon M. Aur. *Med.* 6.13, although I am imagining what he might have said in person.

2. M. Aur. *Med.* 3.18.

3. *SHA, Verus* 10.8.

4. *SHA, Verus* 4.4.

5. *SHA, Verus* 1.4.

6. Attempts have been made to rehabilitate Lucius's character, most recently M. C. Bishop's fine biography, *Lucius Verus and the Roman Defence of the East.*

7. M. Aur. *Med.* 1.17.

8. Fronto to Lucius Verus, 162 A.D., Fronto, *Ep.*, vol. 2.

9. *SHA, Verus* 6.9.

10. *SHA, Verus* 5.8.

11. Fronto to Marcus, 162 A.D., On the Parthian War, sect. 9, Fronto, *Ep.*, vol. 2. Fronto mentions Marcus's having written that anxiety prevented him from reading except in snatches.

12. *SHA, Verus* 7.1.

13. *SHA, Marc.* 8.12.

14. *SHA, Verus* 4.6–7.

15. M. Aur. *Med.* 4.32.

CHAPTER 11. PARTHICUS MAXIMUS

1. Briefing based on M. Aur. *Med.* 7.7, with dialogue invented.

2. Fronto to Lucius Verus, 163 A.D., sect. 3, Fronto, *Ep.*, vol. 2.

3. M. Aur. *Med.* 10.8.

4. Lucius to Fronto, 163 A.D., Fronto, *Ep.*, vol. 2.

5. *SHA, Verus* 7.10.

6. The *Augustan History* claims that Marcus entrusted his daughter to the care of his sister, which seems impossible, as his only sister had been dead for several years. The writer could perhaps have meant one of Lucius's two sisters.

7. Luc. *Hist. conscr.*

8. Cass. Dio 71.2.3; Luc. *Hist. conscr.*

9. *SHA, Verus* 8.3.

10. Eutropius, *Abridgment of Roman History* 8.10.

11. *SHA, Verus* 8.2.

12. Amm. Marc. 6.24.

13. Cass. Dio 71.2.4.

14. Lucius Verus to Fronto, 165 A.D., Fronto, *Ep.*, vol. 2. Lucius does not mention Statius Priscus, though, which might be taken to suggest he had died by this time.

15. Fronto to Lucius Verus, 165 A.D., *Preamble to History,* Fronto, *Ep.*, vol. 2.

16. Luc. *Hist. conscr.*

17. Although Fronto's history was probably never completed or published, Lucian's criticisms seem pertinent.

18. I have to thank M. C. Bishop for pointing out this verbal coincidence, which goes unmentioned by ancient commentators, in *Lucius Verus and the Roman Defence of the East.*

19. M. Aur. *Med.* 6.44.

20. *SHA, Verus* 5.1–6.

21. M. Aur. *Med.* 1.17.

22. *SHA, Marc.* 12.8.

23. Amm. Marc. 6.24.

24. Arr. *Epict. diss.* 3.24.84–87, trans. Long.

25. *SHA, Verus* 8.1, slightly modified.

CHAPTER 12. THE ANTONINE PLAGUE

1. Homer, *Iliad* 1.43–52.

2. Homer, *Iliad*, 1.55.

3. M. Aur. *Med.* 4.48.

4. Amm. Marc. 6.24 ("polluted everything"); Orosius, *History Against the Pagans* 7.15.4.

5. M. Aur. *Med.* 1.4. Exorcisms, as far as we know, were performed by Christians, so this may be a rare allusion by Marcus to his attitude toward that religion.

6. M. Aur. *Med.* 9.2.

7. *SHA, Marc.* 13.6.

8. C. R. Haines, "Note on the Christians," in Marcus Aurelius, *Marcus Aurelius,* ed. and trans. Haines, 386.

9. Cass. Dio 69.3.1.

10. Tertullian, *Apology* 5.

11. Irenaeus, *Against Heresies* 4.30.3, in Roberts, Donaldson, and Coxe, *Ante-Nicene Fathers.*

12. Eusebius, *Ecclesiastical History* 5.1. Roberts, Donaldson, and Coxe, *Ante-Nicene Fathers* 1.305–306, The Martyrdom of Justin Martyr.

13. Pliny, *Letters* X.96–97; Roberts, Donaldson, and Coxe, *Ante-Nicene Fathers* 1.305–306; Herbert Musurillo, *The Acts of the Christian Martyrs* (Oxford: Clarendon, 1972), 42–61 (quote 47).

14. M. Aur. *Med.* 11.3.

CHAPTER 13. THE WAR OF MANY NATIONS

1. Luc. *Alex.* 48.

2. Cass. Dio 72.3.1. The *Augustan History* says that the conflict on the northern frontier broke out while the Parthian War was still in progress, which would appear to mean the autumn of 166 at the latest.

3. Cass. Dio 72.3.1.

4. *SHA, Marc.* 14.1.

5. *SHA, Ant. Pius* 5.4.

6. M. Aur. *Med.* 4.44. Due to the inadequate nature of our evidence, scholars disagree about the date of the Marcomannic invasion. Frank McLynn, among others,

places it in 167, shortly after the Lombardi and Obii incursion, making it a sudden act of treachery following the peace negotiations of Ballomar. Anthony Birley and others place it slightly later, in 170, after the death of Lucius Verus, viewing it in part as retaliation against punitive action taken by Marcus toward the Germanic tribes. Following the initial outbreak of plague, though, despite his own fragile health, Marcus left Italy for the first time, and accompanied Lucius to Pannonia. That suggests the empire faced a military crisis even more dangerous than the Parthian War. There appears to have been a sense of emergency at Rome at this time, which I believe favors the earlier date of 167 for the Marcomannic invasion, and arguably this also better matches the timeline implied by the *Augustan History*.

7. Luc. *Alex.* 48.

8. *SHA, Marc.* 13.2.

9. Luc. *Alex.* 48.

10. *SHA, Verus* 9.7.

11. *SHA, Marc.* 14.1, 14.5.

12. Cass. Dio 72.3.3.

13. The scale of these new measures to secure the Alpine passes is often cited as further evidence against positing a later date for Ballomar's invasion of Italy.

14. Cass. Dio 72.11.1.

15. Cass. Dio 72.11.1; M. Aur. *Med.* 9.42.

16. *SHA, Marc.* 14.5.

17. M. Aur. *Med.* 1.17.

CHAPTER 14. GERMANICUS

1. *SHA, Marc.* 17.4, 21.9.

2. M. Aur. *Med.* 1.17.

3. M. Aur. *Med.* 6.13, 9.36.

4. M. Aur. *Med.* 5.12.

5. *SHA, Marc.* 21.7.

6. *SHA, Marc.* 20.6.

7. Hdn. 1.2.1.

8. M. Aur. *Med.* 9.40.

9. *SHA, Marc.* 17.2.

10. M. Aur. *Med.* 8.37, 9.3.

11. *SHA, Marc.* 3.5.

12. *SHA, Marc.* 17.2.

13. Cass. Dio 72.13.1.

14. Cass. Dio 72.9.1, where the epitomizer Xiphilinus interpolates his own comments.

CHAPTER 15. SARMATICUS

1. This scene based on Cass. Dio 72.7.1, with dialogue invented. A scene based on the battle was at one point intended by screenwriters to be included in the movie *Gladiator* (2000) but after being dropped was later recycled, in another form, for *King Arthur* (2004).

2. M. Aur. *Med.* 2.1.

3. Cass. Dio 72.16.1.

4. *SHA, Marc.* 24.5.

5. *SHA, Marc.* 24.3.

6. Cass. Dio 72.11.1

7. M. Aur. *Med.* 7.3.

8. M. Aur. *Med.* 3.3.

9. M. Aur. *Med.* 10.9.

10. See, e.g., Diogenes Laertius, *Lives of Eminent Philosophers* 7.121. Although, "enslaved person" might be preferable today, I think that the term "slave" plays a role in the literature of Stoic philosophy that justifies retaining that it for the sake of our discussion here.

11. Dio Chrysostom, *Discourses* 14–15.

12. Dio Chrysostom, *Discourses* 15.25, 15.28.

13. M. Aur. *Med.* 10.10.

14. M. Aur. *Med.* 9.29.

15. Birley, *Marcus Aurelius,* 200.

16. Noyen, "Marcus Aurelius, the Greatest Practician of Stoicism," 376.

CHAPTER 16. CASSIUS THE USURPER

1. See Cass. Dio 72.4.1.

2. Cass. Dio 72.4.1.

3. *SHA, Marc.* 26.12.

4. *SHA, Marc.* 25.4. Maecianus's identification seems plausible as he had briefly served as a prefect of Egypt in the past, although the *Augustan History* could be referring to Avidius Maecianus, Cassius's son, who was named after him. See also Jarvis, "Avidius Cassius and Maecianus in the *Historia Augusta*."

5. The precise nature of this office is unclear. Dio says vaguely that at some point after the Parthian War, Marcus ordered Cassius "to have charge of all Asia" (Cass. Dio 72.3.1), meaning everything to the east of the Aegean, and Philostratus likewise refers to Cassius as "the governor of the Eastern provinces" (Philostr. *VS* 2.1.9).

6. In a letter dated April 175, Cassius refers to his election as emperor by the soldiers and promises to look favorably on his "fatherland," the city of Alexandria (Bowman, "A Letter of Avidius Cassius?").

7. M. Aur. *Med.* 1.17; Cass. Dio 72.6.1, 72.24.1; Cass. Dio 72.22.3 ("spitting blood").

8. *SHA, Avid Cass.* 14.1–8.

9. *SHA, Avid. Cass.* 14.5.

10. *SHA, Marc.* 24.9; *SHA, Avid. Cass.* 7.6.

CHAPTER 17. THE CIVIL WAR

1. Scene based on Dio 72.23.1, with dialogue invented.

2. Amm. Marc. 17.12.3.

3. Cassius Dio reports that a portion of them were sent to Britain, although surely this happened after the civil war was over. Dio claims that when Marcus was preparing for the war against Cassius, he "would accept no barbarian assistance, although many nations rushed to offer their services; for he declared that the barbarians ought not to know of the troubles arising between Romans" (Cass. Dio 72.27.1). "Barbarian assistance," however, here must refer to mercenaries fighting for loot under the command of their native chieftains; Marcus evidently did accept many "barbarian" conscripts into auxiliary units under the command of Roman officers.

4. The inscription was found at Ain Zana in Algeria, among the ruins of the Roman city of Diana Veteranorum. Translated in Campbell, *The Roman Army, 31 BC – AD 337*, 64–65.

5. *SHA, Avid. Cass.* 13.3.

6. *SHA, Comm.* 1.9.

7. It may have been an established Stoic political view that a bad ruler was better than a civil war. Plutarch claims that Brutus philosophically questioned potential co-conspirators about their willingness to take part in the assassination of Julius Caesar, including a man called Favonius, who appears to have been a Stoic. Favonius, a "devoted follower of Cato," gave his reason for declining as the belief that "civil war was worse than illegal monarchy," illegal monarchy being a philosophical definition of tyranny (Plutarch, *Life of Brutus*, 12.3). See Sedley, "The Ethics of Brutus and Cassius," for a detailed discussion.

8. Virgil, *Aeneid* 4.173, trans. Fairclough; the speech appears in Cass. Dio 72.24–26.

9. M. Aur. *Med.* 4.49.

10. Speeches and letters quoted in ancient histories, such as the *Augustan History* and Cassius Dio's *Roman History,* are the documents whose authenticity has been questioned most strongly by modern scholarship. Yet Cassius Dio was writing his history within living memory of these events. There would surely have been an outcry from those who knew better if he had completely fabricated the content of such a historic speech, purportedly made in public and forwarded in writing to the Senate. At the least, we might assume that the attribution of the ideas in this speech to Marcus Aurelius, and its overall gist, seemed plausible to most of Dio's readers.

11. M. Aur. *Med.* 9.42.

12. *SHA, Avid. Cass.* 9.2. Marcus returned half their father's property to the sons and daughters of Avidius Cassius, along with gifts of gold and jewels. Alexandria and Druncianus were allowed to travel freely and we are told "they lived not as the children of a pretender but as members of the senatorial order and in the greatest security" (*SHA, Avid. Cass.* 9.4). Marcus took legal action to protect them against insults and they were brought under the protection of his uncle, perhaps the elder Marcus Annius Libo.

CHAPTER 18. THE SETTING SUN

1. *SHA, Marc.* 26.4.

2. Cass. Dio 72.29.1.

3. Cass. Dio 72.30.1.

4. Cass. Dio 72.30.1.

5. As we have seen, the most important client kingdoms on Rome's eastern border were Armenia and Osroene, the latter perhaps the most likely to have sided with Cassius.

6. Cass. Dio 72.30.1.

7. Amm. Marc. 5.5. Luitpold Wallach made the case that the "Antoninus" intended must be Marcus Aurelius on the basis of parallels between the Hebrew texts and Seneca's letters, suggesting that the Jewish author was intentionally drawing upon earlier Stoic sources. See "The Colloquy of Marcus Aurelius with the Patriarch Judah I."

8. *SHA, Marc.* 27.1; Cass. Dio 31.3; on the appointments see Philostr. *VS* 2.2.0.

9. M. Aur. *Med.* 8.14.

10. Cass. Dio 72.32.1.

11. Cass. Dio 72.33.3; *SHA, Avid. Cass.* 3.6–7; Aur. Vict. *Caes.* 16, trans. H. W. Bird.

12. The *Meditations* has an unfinished appearance and contains several references that only Marcus is likely to have understood, such as one to the letter Rusticus sent his mother from Sinuessa. The criticisms, explicit or implicit, of other Romans, such as Hadrian, would also, most likely, have made the volume's content too controversial for Marcus to consider revealing the text to the public.

12. Cass. Dio 72.33.1.

13. Cass. Dio 72.18.1.

14. Cass. Dio 72.20.1.

15. *SHA, Marc.* 24.5, 27.10.

16. Cass. Dio 72.33.1.

17. Aur. Vict. *Caes.* 16.12; Tertullian, *Apology* 25.

18. *SHA, Marc.* 28.1.

19. *SHA, Marc.* 28.4–6, slightly modified.

20. Cass. Dio 72.34.1.

21. Cass. Dio 72.33.1.

22. Cass. Dio 73.1.1.

23. *SHA, Marc.* 28.10.

24. Hdn. 1.3.1; 1.3.4–5.

25. Cass. Dio 72.35.3–4.

EPILOGUE

1. We cannot be certain when the book was completed, although the lack of explicit references to the civil war or to the death of Faustina are clues that it may have

been by early 175. In one passage Marcus may be referring to his wife being pregnant (see M. Aur. *Med.* 9.3).

2. Philostr. *VS* 2.1.9.

3. Cicero, *On the Laws* 2.36; *SHA, Marc.* 27.1.

4. Plato, *Phaedo* 64a.

5. Cornutus, *Greek Theology* 53; M. Aur. *Med.* 4.5, 7.40, 11.6.

Bibliography

Adams, Geoff W. *Marcus Aurelius in the Historia Augusta and Beyond.* Lanham, Md.: Lexington Books, 2014.

Ammianus Marcellinus. *History.* Vol. 1: *Books 14–19.* Trans. J. C. Rolfe. Loeb Classical Library 300. Cambridge: Harvard University Press, 1950.

Apuleius. *Apologia. Florida. De Deo Socratis.* Ed. and trans. Christopher P. Jones. Loeb Classical Library 534. Cambridge: Harvard University Press, 2017.

Arrian. *See* Epictetus.

Birley, Anthony Richard. *Hadrian: The Restless Emperor.* London: Routledge, 2003.

——. *Marcus Aurelius: A Biography.* New York: Routledge, 1966.

Bishop, M. C. *Lucius Verus and the Roman Defence of the East.* Barnsley: Pen & Sword Military, 2018.

Bowman, Alan K. "A Letter of Avidius Cassius?" *Journal of Roman Studies* 60, no. 1 (1970): 21–26.

Brunt, Peter Astbury. *Studies in Stoicism.* Ed. by Miriam Tamara Griffin, Alison Samuels, and Michael Hewson Crawford. Oxford: Oxford University Press, 2013.

Campbell, Brian. *The Roman Army, 31 BC–AD 337: A Source Book.* London: Routledge, 1994.

Cassius Dio. *See* Dio Cassius.

Champlin, Edward. *Fronto and Antonine Rome.* Cambridge: Harvard University Press, 2013.

Cicero. *On the Republic. On the Laws.* Trans. Clinton W. Keyes. Loeb Classical Library 213. Cambridge: Harvard University Press, 1928.

Cooper, Anthony Ashley, Earl of Shaftesbury. *The Life, Unpublished Letters, and Philosophical Regimen of Anthony, Earl of Shaftesbury.* Ed. Benjamin Rand. Online edition. Elibron, 2005.

Cornutus, Lucius Annaeus, *L. Annaeus Cornutus: "Greek Theology," Fragments, and Testimonia.* Trans. George R. Boys-Stones. Atlanta: SBL Press, 2018.

Dio Cassius [Cassius Dio]. *Roman History.* Vol. 9: *Books 71–80.* Trans. Earnest Cary, with Herbert B. Foster. Loeb Classical Library 177. Cambridge: Harvard University Press, 1927.

Bibliography

Dio Chrysostom. *Dio Chrysostom: Discourses 12–30.* Trans. James W. Cohoon. Loeb Classical Library 339. Cambridge: Harvard University Press, 1939.

Diogenes Laertius. *Lives of Eminent Philosophers.* Vol. 2: *Books 6–10.* Trans. R. D. Hicks. Loeb Classical Library 185. Cambridge: Harvard University Press, 1925.

Dryden, John. *The Poems of John Dryden.* Oxford: Oxford University Press, 1958.

Epictetus. *Discourses, Books 1–2.* Trans. W. A. Oldfather. Loeb Classical Library 131. Cambridge: Harvard University Press, 1925.

——. *Discourses: With the Encheiridion and Fragments.* Trans. George Long. London: A. L. Humphreys, 1897.

Eunapius. *Lives of the Philosophers. See* Philostratus.

Eusebius. *Ecclesiastical History.* Vol. 1: *Books 1–5.* Trans. Kirsopp Lake. Loeb Classical Library 153. Cambridge: Harvard University Press, 1926.

Eutropius. *Abridgement of Roman History.* Trans. John Selby Watson. London: Henry G. Bohn, 1853.

Everitt, Anthony. *Hadrian and the Triumph of Rome.* New York: Random House, 2009.

Farquharson, A. S. L., and D. A. Rees. *Marcus Aurelius: His Life and His World.* Oxford: Blackwell, 1951.

Fronto, Marcus Cornelius. *Correspondence.* Vol. 1. Trans. C. R. Haines. Loeb Classical Library 112. Cambridge: Harvard University Press, 1919.

——. *Correspondence.* Vol. 2. Trans. C. R. Haines. Loeb Classical Library 113. Cambridge: Harvard University Press, 1920.

——. *Fronto: Selected Letters.* Trans. Caillan Davenport and Jennifer Manley. London: Bloomsbury Academic, 2014.

Galenus, Claudius. *Galen on the Passions and Errors of the Soul.* Trans. Paul W. Harkins. Columbus: Ohio State University Press, 1963.

Gellius. *Attic Nights.* Vol. 3: *Books 14–20.* Trans. J. C. Rolfe. Loeb Classical Library 212. Cambridge: Harvard University Press, 1927.

Grant, Michael. *The Antonines: The Roman Empire in Transition.* London: Routledge, 1994.

Hadot, Pierre. *The Inner Citadel: "The Meditations" of Marcus Aurelius.* Trans. Michael Chase. Cambridge: Harvard University Press, 2001.

Herodian. *Herodian of Antioch's History of the Roman Empire: From the Death of Marcus Aurelius to the Accession of Gordian.* Trans. Edward C. Echols. Berkeley: University of California Press, 1961.

Bibliography

Historia Augusta. Vol. 1. Trans. David Magie. Rev. David Rohrbacher. Loeb Classical Library 139. Cambridge: Harvard University Press, 2022.

Holiday, Ryan, and Stephen Hanselman. *The Daily Stoic: 366 Meditations on Wisdom, Perseverance, and the Art of Living.* New York: Portfolio/Penguin, 2016.

———. *Lives of the Stoics: The Art of Living from Zeno to Marcus Aurelius.* New York: Portfolio/Penguin, 2020.

Homer. *The Iliad of Homer.* Trans. Samuel Butler. London: Longmans, Green, 1898.

Jarvis, Paul. "Avidius Cassius and Maecianus in the *Historia Augusta*." *Mnemosyne* 68, no. 4 (2015): 666–676. https://doi.org/10.1163/1568525x-12341562.

Jones, C. P. "Aelius Aristides, ΕΙΣ ΒΑΣΙΛΕΑ." *Journal of Roman Studies* 62 (1972): 134–152. https://doi.org/10.2307/298934.

Livy. *History of Rome.* Vol. 1: *Books 1–2.* Trans. B. O. Foster. Loeb Classical Library 114. Cambridge: Harvard University Press, 1919.

Lucian. *Anacharsis or Athletics. Menippus or The Descent into Hades. On Funerals. A Professor of Public Speaking. Alexander the False Prophet. Essays in Portraiture. Essays in Portraiture Defended. The Goddesse of Surrye.* Trans. A. M. Harmon. Loeb Classical Library 162. Cambridge: Harvard University Press, 1925.

———. *How to Write History.* Trans. K. Kilburn. Loeb Classical Library 430. Cambridge: Harvard University Press, 1959.

Marcus Aurelius. *Marcus Aurelius.* Ed. and trans. C. R. Haines. Loeb Classical Library 58. Cambridge: Harvard University Press, 2015.

———. *Marcus Aurelius Antoninus, the Roman Emperor, His Meditations Concerning Himself: Treating of a Natural Man's Happiness Wherein It Consisteth, and the Means to Attain unto It. Translated out of the Orginall Greeke; with notes, by Meric Casaubon.* 1634. Available from Project Gutenberg at https://www.gutenberg.org/files/2680/2680-h/2680-h.htm.

———. *Meditations.* Trans. Gregory Hays. New York: Modern Library, 2002.

———. *Meditations: The Annotated Edition.* Trans. Robin Waterfield. New York: Basic, 2021.

———. *Meditations: The Philosophy Classic.* Trans. George Long. Ed. Donald J. Robertson. Chichester, West Sussex: Capstone, 2020.

———. *Meditations: With Selected Correspondence.* Trans. Robin Hard. Oxford: Oxford University Press, 2011.

———. *Meditations, Books 1–6.* Trans. Christopher Gill. Oxford: Oxford University Press, 2013.

Bibliography

McLynn, Frank. *Marcus Aurelius: A Life*. Cambridge: Da Capo Press, 2009.

Minucius Felix. *Octavius*. *See* Tertullian.

Noyen, P. "Marcus Aurelius, the Greatest Practician of Stoicism." *L'Antiquité classique* 24, no. 2 (1955): 372–383. https://doi.org/10.3406/antiq.1955.3266.

Orosius, Paulus. *Seven Books of History Against the Pagans: The Apology of Paulus Orosius*. Trans. Irving W. Raymond. New York: Columbia University Press, 1936.

Pater, Walter. *Marius the Epicurean*. Oxford: Blackwell, 1973.

Penella, Robert J. *The Private Orations of Themistius*. Berkeley: University of California Press, 2000.

Philostratus. *Lives of the Sophists; Eunapius. Lives of the Philosophers*. Trans. Wilmer C. Wright. Loeb Classical Library 134. Cambridge: Harvard University Press, 1921.

Plato. *Complete Works*. Ed. John M. Cooper and D. S. Hutchinson. Indianapolis: Hackett, 1997.

Pliny the Younger. *Letters*. Vol. 2: *Books 8–10. Panegyricus*. Trans. Betty Radice. Loeb Classical Library 59. Cambridge: Harvard University Press, 1969.

Plutarch. *Lives*. Vol. 3: *Pericles and Fabius Maximus. Nicias and Crassus*. Trans. Bernadotte Perrin. Loeb Classical Library 65. Cambridge: Harvard University Press, 1916.

———. *Lives*. Vol. 6: *Dion and Brutus. Timoleon and Aemilius Paulus*. Trans. Bernadotte Perrin. Loeb Classical Library 98. Cambridge: Harvard University Press, 1918.

Rikkers, Doris, C. I. Scofield, E. Schuyler English, and Arthur L. Farstad. *The Scofield Study Bible: New King James Version*. New York: Oxford University Press, 2002.

Roberts, Alexander, James Donaldson, and A. Cleveland Coxe. *Ante-Nicene Fathers*. Peabody, Mass.: Hendrickson, 1999.

Robertson, Donald. *How to Think Like a Roman Emperor: The Stoic Philosophy of Marcus Aurelius*. New York: St. Martin's, 2020.

———. *Stoicism and the Art of Happiness: Practical Wisdom for Everyday Life*. London: John Murray Learning, 2018.

Ross, Steven K. *Roman Edessa: Politics and Culture on the Eastern Fringes of the Roman Empire, 114–242 C.E.* London: Routledge, 2011.

Sedgwick, Henry Dwight. *Marcus Aurelius. A Biography Told . . . by Letters, Together with Some Account of the Stoic Religion, Etc.* New Haven: Yale University Press, 1921.

Sedley, David. "The Ethics of Brutus and Cassius." *Journal of Roman Studies* 87 (1997): 41–53. https://doi.org/10.2307/301367.

Sellars, John. *Marcus Aurelius*. London: Routledge, Taylor & Francis Group, 2021.

Bibliography

Seneca. *Epistles*. Vol. 1: *Epistles 1–65*. Trans. Richard M. Gummere. Loeb Classical Library 75. Cambridge: Harvard University Press, 1917.

——. *Epistles*. Vol. 2: *Epistles 66–92*. Trans. Richard M. Gummere. Loeb Classical Library 76. Cambridge: Harvard University Press, 1920.

——. *Epistles*. Vol. 3: *Epistles 93–124*. Trans. Richard M. Gummere. Loeb Classical Library 77. Cambridge: Harvard University Press, 1925.

Stanton, G. R. "Marcus Aurelius, Emperor and Philosopher." *Historia: Zeitschrift für alte Geschichte* 18, no. 5 (1969): 570–587.

Stephens, William O. *Marcus Aurelius: A Guide for the Perplexed*. London: Continuum, 2012.

Swain, Simon. "Favorinus and Hadrian." *Zeitschrift für Papyrologie und Epigraphik* 79 (1989): 150–158.

Tertullian. *Apology. De Spectaculis;* Minucius Felix. *Octavius*. Trans. T. R. Glover and Gerald H. Rendall. Loeb Classical Library 250. Cambridge: Harvard University Press, 1931.

Thomas, [Antoine Léonard]. *Eulogium on Marcus Aurelius*. [Trans. D. B. Warden.] New York: Printed for Bernard Dornin, 1808.

Victor, Sextus Aurelius. *A Booklet About the Style of Life and the Manners of the Imperatores: Abbreviated from the Books of Sextus Aurelius Victor*. Trans. Thomas Michael Banchich. Buffalo, N.Y.: Canisius College, 2000.

——. *Liber De Caesaribus of Sextus Aurelius Victor*. Trans. H. W. Bird. Liverpool: Liverpool University Press, 1994.

Virgil. *Eclogues. Georgics. Aeneid: Books 1–6*. Trans. H. Rushton Fairclough. Rev. G. P. Goold. Loeb Classical Library 63. Cambridge: Harvard University Press, 1916.

——. *Virgil's Æneid*. Trans. John Dryden. Harvard Classics, vol. 13. New York: Collier, 1909.

Wallach, Luitpold. "The Colloquy of Marcus Aurelius with the Patriarch Judah I." *Jewish Quarterly Review* 31, no. 3 (1941): 259–286. https://doi.org/10.2307/1452575.

Watson, Paul Barron. *Marcus Aurelius Antoninus*. Freeport, N.Y.: Books for Libraries Press, 1971.

Yourcenar, Marguerite. *Memoirs of Hadrian: And Reflections on the Composition of Memoirs of Hadrian*. Trans. Grace Frick and Marguerite Yourcenar. New York: Farrar, Straus and Giroux, 2005.

Acknowledgments

I would like to thank everyone who helped, including my wife, Kasey Pierce, and my agent, Stephen Hanselman, for their support; and Lalya Lloyd, my freelance editor; James Romm, the series editor; and Susan Laity at Yale University Press for their very detailed and helpful comments on the manuscript.

Index

Index

Index

Index

Index

Ma'nu VIII (king of Osroene), 92, 109, 111

Marcianus, Publius Julius Geminius, 99

Marcius Turbo, 50

Marcomannic War. *See* First Marcomannic War; Second Marcomannic War

Marcomanni tribe, 127, 129, 131, 133, 140, 141–142, 148, 153, 165, 173, 175

Marcus Annius Verus (father of Marcus Aurelius), 14–15, 16, 62

Marcus Annius Verus (grandfather of Marcus Aurelius), 17–18, 44, 50

Marcus Annius Verus (son of Marcus Aurelius), 116, 139

Marcus Aurelius Antoninus: as adopted grandson of Hadrian, 6–7, 49, 51, 65–66; as adopted son of Antoninus Pius, 1, 34, 49, 59; affection for his mother, 9–10, 12–13; in Athens, 182–183; attitude toward slavery, 149–152; auction of imperial treasures, 137–138; in the *Augustan History*, 6, 17, 22, 29, 65, 68, 100, 166, 174, 195; as Caesar, 6, 84–85; character of, 3; childhood tutors, 21–22, 24–27; and China, 114; and the Christians, 123–125; as co-consul, 62–70; as co-emperor, 84–90; correspondence with Fronto, 6, 64, 67, 75, 78–80, 104, 108, 193, 207n11; dealing with enemy captives, 148–149; dealing with the plague, 120, 121–123, 130; on death, 48; death of, 176–177; displays of emotion by, 1–2; and the dying Hadrian, 54–57; early training and education, 18–19, 21–24; and the First Marcomannic War, 141–143, 181; as Germanicus, 143; in Hadrian's villa, 51–52; at the House of Tiberius, 65, 85; as Imperator II, 108; as Imperator III, 112; as Imperator IV, 113; as Imperator V, 133; as Imperator VI, 143; as Imperator VII, 146; as Imperator VIII, 148; insurrection against, 153, 161, 163–169; later tutors, 67–70; leading the Roman army in Pannonia, 132–134; learning from Antoninus Pius, 59–67; on Lucius's flaws, 115; memories of his father, 16; nicknamed Verissimus, 22–23, 27, 33, 199n12; pardoning rebels, 171–172, 213n12; during the Parthian War, 101–102; as Parthicus Maximus, 114; philosophy of life, 3–4; as Pontifex Maximus, 88, 122; portrayals of, 3; as quaestor, 62; return to Rome, 173–174; as senator, 62; and Stoicism, 3–6, 28–30, 53, 63, 79–81, 91, 93, 122, 133, 135, 137, 168; study of philosophy, 26–31, 53, 63–64, 66–70; war with Sarmatians, 145–148. See also *Meditations*

Marius Maximus, 195

Mark Antony, 109, 110

Mars Gravidus (god of marching into war), 19

Martius Verus, 99, 113, 114, 163, 164, 167, 169, 171–172

Mastor (Sarmatian huntsman), 54

Maximus, Claudius, 68, 69

Maximus, Marius, 195

Meander, 138

Meditations: on Antoninus's virtues, 64–66; book 1, 7, 64–66; on death, 125, 177, 184; on deceitful men, 147; English translation, 4; on governing, 51; Hadrian mentioned in, 65–66; Lucius Verus mentioned, 140; on the Marcomannic War, 143; on Marcus's childhood, 31; on Marcus's wartime experience, 174;

Index

Index

Index

Tertullian, 123, 176

Themistius, 73

Therapeutics (Chrysippus), 77

Thrasea (Stoic senator), 83

Tiberius, 65

Trajan, 15, 92, 97, 137

Turbo, Marcius, 50

Ummidius Quadratus, 50

Verus, Gnaeus Julius, 109

Verus, Marcus Annius. *See* Marcus
  Annius Verus (father of Marcus
  Aurelius); Marcus Annius Verus
  (grandfather of Marcus Aurelius);
  Marcus Annius Verus (son of
  Marcus Aurelius)

Verus, Publius Martius, 99, 113, 114, 163,
  164, 167, 169, 171–172

Vespasian, 158

Victor, Aurelius, 175, 176

Victorinus, Aufidius, 152, 176

Victorinus, Furius, 98, 100, 131, 134

Victory (goddess), 142

Vologases IV (king of Parthia), 91,
  92–97, 100, 109, 111, 113, 206n6

Volucer (Lucius's horse), 105–106

Wa'el (king of Osroene), 109

War of Many Nations. *See* First Marcomannic War

Xiphilinus (Byzantine scribe), 142

Yourcenar, Marguerite, 7

Zanticus (Iazyx chieftain), 147, 165

Zeno, 25, 80